D0581715

'Teddy is such a lucky little boy to have Elle as his mummy. I have no doubt that he is so proud of the way Elle speaks about him and honours him in all that she does. A beautiful book, from a wonderful woman, about a very special little boy'

GIOVANNA FLETCHER

'*Ask Me His Name* has touched me like no other book has ever done. I did not want to put it down until it was finished. An incredibly powerful, raw, honest and emotional story of a wonderful family and the heartbreaking loss of their beautiful baby boy, Teddy, told through the words of his loving mum. This book will stay with you long after you have put it down'

JOOLS OLIVER

'It takes a huge amount of courage to re-integrate into the world again after your anticipated version of motherhood has been so brutally and painfully ripped away from you. Yet fuelled by the love of Teddy, Elle has managed to transform her pain into power – becoming a beacon of healing light for all, which is so very much needed in this world'

ANNA LEWIS (SKETCHYMUMA)

'To be able to openly share the unthinkable and write about Teddy with such truth, honesty, beauty and humour takes huge courage. This is such an important book that spoke to me on so many levels – it will give you a deeper understanding about the reality of grief and the true meaning of a mother's love'

IZZY JUDD, BESTSELLING AUTHOR OF *DARE TO DREAM*

'Though heartbreaking in places, *Ask Me His Name* is a remarkably uplifting tale of a mother's love for her son who was born but could not stay. By offering such a raw and honest insight into what happened, Elle opens up the conversation and this in turn helps us all to not be afraid to say something – anything! – to parents who have lost children, when we might otherwise have said nothing at all. This is such an important read and it must have taken an extraordinary amount of courage to write and share the most personal of stories with the world'

SARAH TURNER (THE UNMUMSY MUM)

'Bold, compelling and heartwrenchingly honest, this story of how humans can cope in the darkest of hours will blow you away'

MARINA FOGLE

A Mother's Story of Hope

Ask
Me
His
Name

Learning to live and laugh again
after the loss of my baby

Elle Wright

Published by Lagom
An imprint of Bonnier Books UK
2.25, The Plaza,
535 Kings Road,
Chelsea Harbour,
London, SW10 0SZ

www.bonnierbooks.co.uk

Hardback – 978-1-788-700-34-4
Ebook – 978-1-788-700-33-7

A CIP catalogue of this book is available from the British Library.

Typeset by Envy Design Ltd

Illustration on p. 304 © Charlotte Peach

Printed and bound in Great Britain by Clays Ltd, Elcograf S.p.A.

3 5 7 9 10 8 6 4 2

A portion of the proceeds from the sale of this book will be donated to
Tommy's charity. Reg. (1060508)

For Nico, my darling husband; who loves me
(and puts up with me!) like no one else could.

And for Boris, who helped me learn to smile again,
when I thought I never would.

Contents

Introduction

I'M ELLE, WELL ELEANOR, BUT EVERYONE HAS COME TO CALL ME ELLE FOR THE MOST PART, APART FROM MY PARENTS AND A FEW CLOSE FAMILY MEMBERS. My mum loves my name and refuses to shorten it, as she insists she didn't give me, 'Such a beautiful name for it to be shortened!' That's fine by me, I'll answer to anything – many of the names not-so-nice when you have older brothers! Ah, yes, older brothers, of which I have two. I grew up in Dorset and, via London, have ended up in Surrey, where I live with my husband, Nico. We have a son, Teddy, but his story is a little different as he never got to come home with us after he was born, as he died at just three days old. I found myself catapulted into a narrative of motherhood that I never expected, one that I was terrified of living in. No one had warned me that this could happen; this wasn't how it was supposed to be. I didn't know how we would carry on being 'normal' without Teddy here, or how we would parent him, or how everyone would treat us – but, so far, it seems to have worked out OK.

That's why I am writing this book – to tell you that becoming a parent isn't always the journey we expect it to be, and to share with you my unexpected path into motherhood. It's a route that I hope no one else has to walk, but sadly I know that they do. So I am sharing our story to help them feel less like the only ones, and to hopefully help other people understand a little more about what being Teddy's mum has been like for me. Think of it as a parenting manual for the unlucky. (Yes, you'll also find lots more bad jokes here.)

So, this is me. I don't know why you have picked this book up – maybe it's because you're in this boat too, or maybe it's because you want to help someone who is. Whatever your reason, I hope this goes a little way to help.

Chapter 1

In the Beginning

I HAD A FANTASTIC CHILDHOOD, AND I REALISE I AM INCREDIBLY LUCKY TO GET TO SAY THAT. I can't really recall any bad memories, other than when my dear grandad passed away very suddenly when I was ten years old. The rest of my childhood was filled with lots of laughter, brilliant family holidays and occasional (OK, daily) bickering with my brothers.

I am the youngest of three, and my brothers are both older than me by at least four years. I think that being one of three children always made me think I would go on to be the mother of three children too. My mum was (and still is) so loving and nurturing; always taking time to encourage us in the things we were passionate

3

about and never laughing off our ideas or telling us we couldn't try something. I always remember thinking my dad was super fun; whether it was because he rugby tackled us in the garden or threw us around in the pool on holiday, or the way he drove faster over bumpy roads to hear our squeals of excitement in the back of the car. That and it was the 1980s/early 1990s so he was always wearing Ray-Bans, and to me that made him legitimately supercool.

I always felt much younger than my brothers, as they were *so* close in age – my mum had two under two by the time she was twenty-five. Being the youngest isn't always the easiest. I think it's because I spent much of my formative years being told, 'You can't join in because...' (insert you're 'too small'/'too young'/'a girl', here). From a young age, I learnt to assert myself to ensure I would be included. This often resulted in my poor mum having to retrieve a three-year-old me from the highest piece of play equipment in a playground after I had inevitably got stuck – and the harsh reality set in that I was indeed 'too small' to join in with many things.

That said, I have always been close to my brothers, and I love them both dearly, and although we are still always squabbling, and are all very different people, we share the same common ground of our sense of humour. Taking the piss out of each other, and others, is the very foundation upon which our sibling relationship has thrived for over three decades. It's what we enjoy most!

I am not sure if it is just me out of the three of us that looks back over these years with such rose-tinted spectacles, but I honestly couldn't think of an upbringing I would rather have had. We lived and grew up in the same house from as young as I can remember, as I had been just three years old when we moved in. My parents still live there now, although it has changed a lot, and thankfully the pale peach leather 1980s' sofas made their exit years ago. We lived in a village in Dorset, and all attended schools nearby. Most of my friends lived in the same village – many are still there. As much as I loved it, it did strike me as a 'You'll never leave' kind of place and for that reason, for me anyway, I just always knew I *had* to get out. That said, I do love going 'home, home' to see my parents, and I visit them often, but there is always that fear of bumping into people from years gone by who I rather wouldn't make the time for idle chit-chat with (there, I said it!).

Fast forward to my early twenties and I was living and working not far from my parents, in Bournemouth, and was fairly happy with my life choices so far. I was managing a spa in a beautiful hotel, a job I loved, and I was living right near the beach, as well as close to my friends. Ideal.

I met my husband in 2008 at the office he worked in, by chance really. One of my clients at the spa had become more of a friend (in fact, she's very much a best friend all these years later), and she was in desperate need of having her nails done before a night out. So, I agreed to pop over to her office after I had finished work as she was so busy. I rang the buzzer and was let into the building where I proceeded to make my way upstairs to meet her.

When I arrived, I was greeted by a huge, empty but pretty spectacular office, with two guys sitting at their desks with headphones on. I awkwardly gestured towards one of them as if to say 'Please help me' with a panicked face. For a moment, I thought I might have got the wrong place/date/time? Then guy number one took his headphones off and said if I could sit over on the sofas then my friend would be out of a meeting pretty soon. I did as I was told.

Turns out that guy number two – the one who didn't

take his headphones off and just stared at me blankly – is now my husband. I learned a couple of years later, after I had actually been on a few dates with him, that he actually said to his colleague, after I had walked over to the other side of the office, 'Who the hell is she? I'd marry her tomorrow.' All of his friends make a huge joke of this now and it was even mentioned in his wedding speech. I am guessing the lesson he probably believes that has been learnt here is: be careful what you wish for…

We didn't just miraculously get together after that awkward first office meet. I had a boyfriend at the time, albeit a rather shit one, but a boyfriend I lived with nonetheless. Nico had recently moved to the area and had had various girlfriends in that timeframe too, I believe. (I am aware that makes him sound successful with the ladies, and I am probably doing him a huge favour here!) We both carried on as we were and I think I saw him at a few social occasions that had been organised by my friend. I always suspected he was very shy, or just rude, perhaps! If only I had known he just wanted to marry me, hey?

Fast forward again to August 2010. I was single, he was single, and on a (very) random night out in a questionable bar in Bournemouth there he was, standing at the bar with his friends. We chatted for a while and I thought nothing more of it. Until the next day, of course, when my friend texted me to explain that he had apparently come into work waxing lyrical about just how long he had chatted to me at the bar the previous evening. She told me I should go on a date with him. I said no.

The following week we had a girls' night down on Sandbanks Beach in Poole on a Thursday evening; a prosecco-fuelled event where I was enjoying a wonderful night watching the summer fireworks. He came to save the day with some more prosecco (I'll be honest, at this point this was the last thing I needed), and we chatted and watched the conveniently timed meteor shower that the universe laid on for us. Miraculously, drunk me managed not to make an utter tit of myself (well, actually, I think maybe I did, but he's a forgiving kind of guy!) and the following day he texted me and asked me to dinner. A week or so later, on 19th August 2010, we had our first date at a beautiful sea-front restaurant.

After that, we were pretty much always together. Something just clicked that evening at dinner, and as I drove home that evening after he had said goodbye with a simple kiss on my cheek, I knew he was also an utter gentleman. I don't think I have ever chatted so much to someone and found so much common ground. The poor waiter had to come to our table about five times to try and take an order before either of us had even looked at the menu!

Our relationship was unlike any other I had ever had; we didn't argue or bicker, we just got on really well. We still do to this day. Perhaps it is because we are both one of three children and both the youngest; we have endured the teasing and the hand-me-downs. Or perhaps it is just because we are so different in character. He always knows how to calm me down, and cheer me up. He'll run me a bath when I have had a tough day. It just works. It still amazes me that despite how very different our personalities are, we just have the same thoughts on so many subjects. I'm fiery and opinionated; he's calm and collected. I walk into a room and start cracking jokes; he surveys the situation and speaks to everyone politely. That's us in a nutshell. Most importantly our vision for our life together, the family life we both wanted to strive for, was the same. Our values are just the same, he just got me, and I felt so incredibly lucky that he did.

We moved in together the following May (after two tester holidays), and the next year, at the end of 2012, we moved to London to live and work. This was a brilliant time in our lives. Although I initially hated London when we arrived (new places, new job and few friends there), once I got into the swing of things I loved it; I think we both did. I am really glad we lived there for two years, it was like a major bucket-list item had been ticked off. It made me feel more worldly wise somehow, because it was a million miles away from the rural village life I had grown up in, and the laid-back coastal living I had become accustomed to. Our work hours were longer, our social engagements never-ending. I was going out almost every night, from Tuesday onward, which seemed perfectly socially acceptable. I made some brilliant new friends there, who I am happy to say are friends for life. One thing remained consistent though – my relationship with Nico. We were growing together, doing all of these exciting things together, and it was brilliant.

It was after living and working in London for eight months that we got engaged. On Friday, 5th June 2013, we headed back down to Bournemouth for a weekend with friends. He left work early (a miracle in itself, I should have known something was up) and we were back in Bournemouth in time to pick up fish and chips and head down to Sandbanks Beach for the sunset. Just as we got up to leave, it was there, on that very same stretch of beach that drunken me had almost ruined this one before it even got off the ground, that he got down on one knee and presented me with a beautiful sparkler while asking me to be his wife.

We got married ten months later, on 19th April 2014, in a church just down the road from his parents' house, and we had a marquee reception for our guests back at their family home. It was perfect, although I am pretty sure most people say that about their wedding day. Even now, I look at photographs of that day and I can't believe how happy I was. I can remember looking at those photos about six months after Teddy had died and asking myself, *I wonder if I will ever feel that deliriously happy again in my life?* I do hope so.

We honeymooned on the West Coast of America, starting in San Francisco and driving down the coast in a convertible Mustang. We stopped in various places, took in some breath-taking sights and ate far too much – exactly as you should do on honeymoon I suppose. I can recall us saying to each other that we wanted to do one action-packed trip together before we had children, a holiday of driving and doing exactly as we pleased before the back seat was filled with crying, whinging and 'Are we there yet?' We agreed that with a holiday like this we would really go out from our life as a couple with a bang!

We talked a lot on that holiday about starting a family and when we would start 'trying'. I had turned 29 two days after we got married, the day we had left for honeymoon, and my husband was due to turn 29 later that year. We felt that we had plenty of time – we had friends and family members who'd had children in their thirties so we weren't in a huge rush. We knew we both wanted a family and that was the most important thing to us. I couldn't envisage our lives without one.

★

First things first, we had to find the perfect family home. We began our hunt upon our return from honeymoon but, as much as we loved London, we couldn't afford a house. We could have just about afforded a flat the size of the one we were living in, if we changed locations and were prepared to get something that needed a bit of work. We weren't afraid of a project, in fact we both very much wanted one, but we didn't want to end up somewhere we would feel crammed in like sardines when a baby did come along. We wanted a house. So, we began to spread our net a little further afield. We looked at all of the train lines heading into

London (from the south, as both sets of parents lived in that direction) and we worked out how quickly we could both get into London – Nico's job was in Central London and, even though I was based at home, I regularly travelled all over the UK and into London.

After much deliberation, we settled on a small market town in Surrey – a beautiful historical little place – and from May onwards we looked at so many houses. We decided to keep open minds and not rule anything out, so we looked at lots of things that were highly impractical (or downright ugly), and by the end of August we had found 'the one'. We got our mortgage in principle, our offer was accepted and our dreams of owning a house on the dreamiest Victorian street you ever did see were coming to life! Well, I can tell you that a full building survey put an end to that, when the surveyor told us that the house had subsidence and we should probably drop our offer considerably if we didn't want to end up with the house falling down somewhere along the line. By the middle of October the whole thing had fallen through and we were heartbroken. Back to square one.

Now I am a big believer in fate. The estate agent had kept telling us that houses on this particular street didn't come up for sale; in fact, it had been almost two years since the last one had been bought and sold on that dreamy street. I think this is why we had fallen harder for that first house, we *had* to have it. After it all went tits-up we moped for a few days, but the following week Nico called me from work and I could sense the excitement in his voice straight away.

'Elle, the agent has just called me. A house on the other side of the road about two doors up is coming on the market.'

We have to buy it! That was my first thought. I didn't care, I didn't want to see it, I just wanted to buy that bloody house.

The following day I was on my way back to London from a work trip to Sussex, and I drove to see the house. I drove up that dreamy little street and I pulled my car up and parked as close as I could to that house – it was raining and dark and I had to get as good a view as possible. Now I know this all makes me sound utterly creepy, but we were under pressure and time was of the essence. House buying does strange things to you! The competitive side of me had to get this house – it's the same feeling that comes over me when I spend too much time on eBay! – and I wasn't about to let someone else get it. As I sat in my car and stared at that house (yes, still being creepy), a sense of warmth and knowing came over me. I knew I wanted to live in this street, it felt like I had been here before, like it was a really familiar place that I knew well. I went home to Nico that Friday evening and said, 'Yes, we have to have it.' By the end of the following day our offer had been accepted and the vendors said they wanted a quick sale and could be out within six weeks – meaning that we could be in by Christmas.

We actually first stepped into the house the following weekend, after we had the sale agreed and the mortgage approved. Luckily for us it was even better than the first house across the street that we had fallen so hard for. It had a bigger hallway, beautiful period features and it just felt 'right'. I couldn't wait to move in, and crossed my fingers that we really would be in by Christmas so that we could start to think about the family we both wanted.

We moved in on Saturday, 13th December 2014. Our chapter living in London was over and I couldn't have been happier. I could hear my footsteps when I walked up our street in the evening back from the train station; nothing else, just my feet touching the ground. No sirens, nor shouting, nor traffic. This was the peaceful, family-friendly setting we had been hoping for.

Now you might very well wonder, why has she gone into so much detail about this house? It is this house, this home, that has largely saved me in many of my darkest hours after Teddy died. I have poured my heart, soul and every ounce of creativity into these walls. It's a sanctuary in more ways than I could even put into words, which is so strange when I think back to myself sitting in the car staring at it through a rainy car window on a cold October evening and wishing it was mine. I truly believe that it is this house that enabled me to start to let the light in again. It gave me the courage to start to try and be myself again, it wrapped itself around me when I needed it the most and gave me a place to focus my mind, perusing a passion that I had rarely had time to indulge in when I was at work.

Once we moved into the house, the renovation began almost immediately (sorry, Nico!). Within a week I had ripped up floors in the bathroom and the kitchen, we were measuring up for various changes and our life was filled with excitement and change. After a break for Christmas, we were straight back to 'nest building'. We were so busy in the house, getting everything how we wanted it and trying to undo all the mistakes (in my opinion!) the previous owners had made.

I call it nest building because that's exactly what we were doing; we had made the decision, as the house sale was going through, that now was the time to start trying for a baby. Even though we were both under 30 (me just!), we thought it could take some time to conceive as in 2012 I had been diagnosed with intermittent PCOS (polycystic ovaries syndrome), which means my stress levels affect how my ovaries choose to behave. We wanted to give ourselves time to plan for a family as we knew it probably wouldn't happen overnight for us. Regardless of how long I feared it might take, I was ready to be a mummy.

In January, I started work as a sales manager for one of the biggest beauty brands there is (*cough* because I'm worth it *cough*). I immersed myself in my new role, travelling into London most days again, and in the work we were doing in the house. As soon as it was Monday, I blinked and Friday had rolled around. The weekends went by in a blur of DIY. We used all our spare time and money getting things done in the house.

After a couple of months I was exhausted, and not really looking after myself. I always ate fairly well but I just didn't feel that well. I guzzled down coffees to get me through my working week and often found myself too busy to eat properly. Although I loved the buzz of my job and the brand I was working for, I had put my well-being well and truly on the back burner.

I tried to address this through a new addition to my family – and I don't mean a baby. In mid-March 2015, we were joined by the other true love of my life: Boris the pug. Oh, how I had longed for Boris. For as long as I could remember, I didn't just need a dog, I needed a pug. He certainly needed a lot of care and attention, but he brought true joy into our lives, and he was such a good distraction from work and the DIY. Also, good preparation for a baby, I thought.

By our seventh month of trying, I still hadn't fallen pregnant. I had been so busy with the first whirlwind five months of the year that I hadn't really had time to get too upset about it. I had celebrated my 30th birthday and we had had our first wedding anniversary. Lots of champagne had been consumed and we had been having a wonderful time. Once all of the celebrations were over, though, I think it hit me. Why weren't we falling pregnant?

Was I just being impatient? Three close friends of mine had started trying for a baby around the same time; all three were now pregnant. Two of them I half-expected to be pregnant quickly as it wasn't their first baby, but the other friend, surely, she had as much chance as me? Why was I the only one still not expecting?

I tried to put it to the back of my mind, but that proves a difficult task when every five minutes you seem to be confronted with a well-meaning comment from friends or family of 'So you'll be starting a family soon then?' or 'Can we expect the pitter-patter of tiny feet soon?' I had to switch off from it all. Focus on work, focus on the house and on my relationship, which I certainly didn't want it to start putting a strain on. My close friends knew it was touchy subject, so thankfully they just stopped asking for the progress report on how things were going in that department. In my mind, it was fairly self-evident how things were going...

During the months that followed I decided to make a few lifestyle changes in order to help myself to increase my chances of falling pregnant. I stopped drinking all the coffees that the world had to offer – by this I mean I cut down to one a day. I did lots of research into fertility foods and the things that you should cut out and tried to follow them as best I could. I didn't drink alcohol before Thursday during the week; if I could make it to Thursday without having that glass of wine or a G & T then I was surely doing myself some good? They were all just little changes.

Having Boris helped too, as now it was the summer and the evenings were lighter, I could take him out on a long walk every evening – pugs hate the heat, evening walks in the summer are the only way! This was doing me more good than him. I was actually taking time at the end of my day to stop looking at my work laptop/iPad/phone and walk away from it all. Plus, I was getting exercise again, albeit gentle exercise, but something that wasn't just me charging from meeting to meeting. I finally felt relaxed and started to stress a little less about trying to be pregnant.

At the time, all of the changes we were making in the house were with family life in mind. I can remember constantly saying to Nico, 'When the baby comes though, we'll put this here.' Every time we changed or moved something, it was on my mind. I guess that is probably quite a natural instinct when you are hoping for a family – you are always looking ahead and seeing the vision of your future selves (and extra mini-selves) and planning for how that will work; what the dynamics will be like. It was no different for us when making changes to the house – I wanted to make sure it was just right for whatever little people came into the picture.

The changes I made to my lifestyle finally paid off and on 22nd September 2015, we found out I was pregnant. We were going to be parents; our wish had finally come true! I remember the day in so much detail. It was a Tuesday and my father-in-law's birthday, so we had arranged to go out for dinner that evening to celebrate. Nico and I were both off work that week; we both needed a break and had agreed we would take a week off to try and get some more work done in the overgrown garden. (It seems that when you buy a house with a fairly sizeable garden as first-time buyers that you generally completely underestimate the enormity of the task in hand, and indeed the time it will take to complete. We have learnt a simple formula now of estimating the time we think it will take us and then multiplying that by about ten. Therefore, if you believe something will take you a weekend to complete, fully expect to spend weekends working on that project for the next two and a half months of your life!)

We had been out in the garden the day before, the Monday. Ripping out shrubs and cutting back overgrown ivy. I was shattered, but I thought it was probably from work. I had been working non-stop up to that week off and I needed a break, mentally and physically. After lunch, I said to Nico that I was going to just listen to my body and have a lie-down. I slept for the rest of that afternoon, which was completely out of character for me – I have never been (and am still not) a napper. I felt like I had been hit by a ton of bricks.

I had already done two pregnancy tests earlier in the month; one just before we went to a friend's wedding (as I didn't want to hit the gin if I was indeed pregnant) which was about four weeks into my cycle, and the other the week before I had been off work. Both negative. Having PCOS meant I often had long cycles, usually 35 days or so, but they were sometimes even longer. I wasn't ever really sure when my period was coming, I just waited for it to come.

The following morning, after a 10 hour sleep, I woke up *still* feeling tired. It had been a really warm night and we had the bedroom window open. All I could smell was lavender, like someone had forcefully shoved a bunch under my nose – really strong lavender. I looked out of the window feeling slightly as though I was losing my marbles. Sure enough, I had cut my lavender back the previous weekend. There was none. I looked to the right of our garden, nothing. Then I looked to the left – two gardens down I could see an enormous lavender bush growing in my neighbour's front garden; still flourishing and covered in the last busy bees of the season. *No*, I thought to myself, *That cannot be what I can smell. Can it?*

I could remember reading something about a heightened sense of smell sometimes being an early sign of pregnancy. Then I thought about yesterday's bout of inescapable tiredness, and how even now I was *still* tired. I scrabbled around in my underwear drawer for the last of the pregnancy tests from a pack I had bought the previous week. I rushed to the bathroom and peed on that stick faster than I have ever wanted to pee on anything in my life. As I sat and waited, staring blankly at that little stick, sure enough that second line appeared. Clear as day. Almost six weeks since the first day of my last period – a positive pregnancy test!

I ran downstairs to tell Nico, only to remember that the reason I had woken up was because he had alerted me to his early morning trip to the local rubbish-tip that he was making (story of our lives, by the way). He was out. I had the most exciting news in the whole bloody world, and he was out?! I ran back upstairs and grabbed my mobile in an effort to call him straight away. Only to watch it out of the corner of my eye flashing on the bedside table. Great.

It must have only been half an hour or so, but waiting for him to get home felt like a lifetime. As I heard the door go I ran downstairs with a beaming smile. I had got myself up, showered and dressed – I wanted to look half decent for this momentous occasion! As I greeted him at the front door he said, 'Wow, you're up. I thought you were going to have a big lie-in as you were so tired?'

I was beaming from ear to ear and replied, 'Close your eyes and open your hands.' It's a little thing my grandma used to say to us when we were children before she gave us a treat! He rolled his eyes and obliged. I placed the positive pregnancy test into the palm of his hand.

As he opened his eyes I could see the expression change on his face as the penny dropped – as he realised what he was looking at. He began beaming, and I began to cry. I never thought anything could have topped our wedding day for that feeling of elation, yet here we were. We were going to be parents. We were both speechless, completely and utterly over the moon. That evening we went out for dinner at our favourite Italian restaurant with my in-laws and they guessed straight away when I said no to a glass of red. They cried, we cried; all was good with the world and I couldn't have been happier.

Chapter 2

All Change

I FOUND PREGNANCY WENT RELATIVELY EASY ON ME
– THAT SOUNDS SMUG, I KNOW. When I think about
my pregnancy and birth story in comparison to those
of my friends and acquaintances, I feel lucky. I was
what my sister-in-law would refer to frequently as 'a
pregnancy unicorn'. We had wanted for this pregnancy
to happen, so badly, like *so* many couples, that I
wanted to try and embrace the changes in my body
and enjoy the feelings and emotions of pregnancy (that
and eating, I wanted to enjoy *all* of the eating).

We found out I was pregnant just before I was
six weeks; this is relatively late I think, as many of
my friends seemed to know even before the four-

week mark. This was down to my mixed-up, lengthy cycles and the fact that the previous tests had all been negative. I honestly didn't believe my luck on that final test when that second line appeared. I kept holding it up to the light and performing over-exaggerated and elongating blinks to 'reset' my eyes, thinking that when I looked again it would be just one line.

I was bursting with excitement, bursting to tell people. We told our parents straight away, and then a handful of very close friends when I was about nine weeks along. I'll be honest, I didn't really consider the risk of miscarriage; silly, now I think back. In my head, from the moment we found out, that was it – we were going to be parents. It was like my positive thinking wouldn't allow me to even consider losing a pregnancy, which is ridiculous as now I know the statistics on miscarriage I think I will fear for the worst in every future pregnancy. The reason we waited until 12 weeks and our first scan to tell most people was because I didn't quite believe it was real. I couldn't believe it myself until I actually *saw* it for myself. I can remember feeling so nervous when we arrived for our first scan – that feeling of nervousness and excitement that swelled up inside me, and I didn't know whether to squeal with excitement or retire into the corner of the waiting room to cry.

Our scan was on a Monday morning. Nico came with me and we arranged that afterwards I would drop him into work, before my first meeting of the day in London. The scan felt like the most magical experience. We got to see our little baby floating around in there – kicking and wriggling, so full of life. It was real; *so very real.* I couldn't wait to tell people. I hurriedly took snaps of our scan pictures on my phone so that I could send them straight to my mum and my closest friends. Our baby, just hanging out in there, safe and sound. Listening to that heartbeat for the first time was incredible. I felt a wave of emotion surge through me; a feeling of happiness that I couldn't quite explain and still can't really. When I dropped my husband off at work I remember getting a text from him a little later that read, 'This is the greatest Monday morning ever. I wish all Monday's could feel this good.' I thought to myself, *So do I.*

Once we had told a few more people, the excitement really set in, as I am sure it does for most expectant couples. People started asking us 'So, will you find out what you're having?' and 'Have you thought of any names yet?' It felt so lovely to know that other people were as excited and positive as we were. I often wonder if I'll ever feel that excited or positive about another pregnancy, if we are lucky enough to be blessed with one. Have I been entirely robbed of that wonderful feeling, that blissful naivety that engulfs you and makes you walk around with a knowing smile that you are about to bring a new life into the world? I really, sincerely hope not. Those months were so enjoyable for me – even trying to juggle the pregnancy hormones with the exhaustion of work, and trying to shoehorn myself into any item of clothing that still fit.

We decided unanimously that we wouldn't find out the sex of the baby at the next scan. Neither of us needed to know. There was a chance that I might need a caesarean section because of some previous medical history, so I was having extra scans and was under close care of an obstetrician for the duration of the pregnancy. For me, I suppose, knowing that there was a chance we would know the exact date the baby would arrive meant I definitely didn't want to know the sex too. Where would be the element of surprise? Would I just be left to announce a weight and a name?

I know that there are lots of people who get great comfort in knowing all of these things and naming their baby before his or her entrance into the world. For me it felt too regimented, too planned. We had planned long enough to try and have this baby; so, for the first time in my life (ever) I decided to simply go with the flow. That felt good. When people asked 'So, what are you having?', with the assumption that all pregnant women in 2016 must have decided to determine the sex of their baby before birth, I simply (and quite annoyingly, I must admit) said, 'A baby. I'm having a baby.' I can tell you that one really pisses people off, just in case you're after any tips.

We thought about names *a lot*. I say 'we', I most definitely mean 'I'. Traditional names all appealed to me so much more than others. Both my husband and I have traditional names; he is Nicholas George (shortened to Nico as a baby, but definitely not Greek as so many people assume!) and I am Eleanor Frances (named after two aunts from both sides of the family). I can remember writing names down in lists in my phone, then going back into those lists and deleting them here and there once I had totally gone off them. That was the risk – I didn't want to 'go off' my firstborn child's name. I put so much thought and effort into those names, writing them in combinations with different middle names. Although there were far more girls' names on the list than boys' (girls' names seemed so much prettier, with so much more choice!), I was convinced I was having a boy. There were three front-runners on the boys' list, all of which my husband and I loved, and one of which came to be used.

Of course, when you are thinking of names, every single person wants to put their name into the hat, well not their name as such, but a name they think would be suitable. Why anyone, no matter how close to you they are, would think you would just allow them to name your firstborn child on your behalf is beyond me. 'Oh, yeah sure, I'm not really fussed, so you go ahead and name the baby,' said no expectant mother, ever. People are just trying to be nice, be involved and get excited with you. The biggest fear is always that you'll reel off some of your name ideas only to be met with horrified faces or a really fake grimace of a smile that tells you they've virtually had to hold themselves back from shouting, 'That's awful! Why would you name a child that?' So, after a while, I stopped sharing my ideas.

Teddy's name had both sentiment and family connections behind it. His full name, Edward Constantine, had been on the list since I was about nine weeks' pregnant, floating up there in the top of my ideas. Nico's grandfather on his mother's side had been Edward, and was always called Ted. My brother is called Edward, but has always been Ed, or Eddie when we were younger. Edward is a real family name on both sides, and a name we both loved, but we knew if we used it then any little boy we had would always be Teddy. I felt as though it was a name that could be used equally as a name for a little boy as for a grown-up; a name that wouldn't sound out of place being shouted across a classroom, or across a pub or a rugby pitch. The middle name Constantine came from our love of the North Cornish coastline, and in particular Constantine Bay. It really is one of those beaches that always takes my breath away whenever we visit, come rain or shine. We had both fallen in love with that bay during our many trips to Cornwall, and we knew it would be a place that we forever visited as a family. As a middle name, I felt it was the perfect mix of traditional and unusual. It's a name I will almost certainly use again, too. I simply love it.

As Christmas 2015 approached, my stomach swelled and I began to look most definitely pregnant (as opposed to the 'I have over-eaten' look). We celebrated Nico's 30th birthday at the beginning of December, and we celebrated a whole year in our first proper 'home' that we had worked so hard to get. By Christmas Day I was exactly 19 weeks' pregnant, and we were due to have our 20-week scan just after New

Year. I hadn't made any social media announcements in relation to being pregnant yet, and although our friends, family and work colleagues knew, that wider 'Facebook audience' hadn't a clue about our impending arrival. So, on Christmas Day, as we returned home from a wonderful day at my parents-in-law's, I changed into my leggings and comfy jumper and posed next to our Christmas tree for a perfectly festive announcement. I posted the photo on Instagram and shared it to my Facebook page. I can remember the comments of congratulations coming in thick and fast. That was it, we had told the world we were going to be parents.

We spent a quiet (and sober) New Year in Cornwall with my parents-in-law at their newly acquired family holiday home. I can recall our entire stay being filled with chatter of 'When we bring the baby here we can . . .' and 'Won't it be fun to walk down to the beach with the baby'. The next time we visited there would be three of us (well four, if you count Boris the pug). It was all too exciting. I scoffed fudge and pasties like there was no tomorrow – there was certainly no denying how pregnant I was beginning to look.

I went back to work in January with a spring in my step. It was funny to think that I only had three and a half months left before I went on maternity leave. Teddy's due date was towards the end of May, so I had decided to finish work mid-April. My job as a sales manager involved me driving around most days, being stuck in heavy traffic for long periods of time, in and around London. Some days I could do upwards of seven hours of driving, and that was starting to make me really tired, as much as I tried to fight it. If I wasn't in the car, I was on trains and Tubes in Central London, lugging bags of products and my laptop from meeting to meeting. So, finishing up a little earlier and giving myself four weeks at home before the baby arrived seemed like the most sensible idea.

Our 20-week scan was textbook. The baby was doing really well, all of the measurements and the results of the anomaly scan were good. We heard the heartbeat again and my heart sang with pride. All was going swimmingly.

When I was 22 weeks' pregnant we met up with my parents to buy the pram. It was the first thing we bought. My mum and dad had wanted to buy it for us, as they had been given a pram by their parents for my eldest brother's arrival in 1979. I think they were both as excited as we were as we went into John Lewis and Mothercare searching for 'the one'. It was actually one of my most enjoyable memories of pregnancy, shopping for our baby's pram with my parents. I could see how excited they were and how much they wanted to help us out. It made me feel so very lucky indeed.

A week later I experienced my first pregnancy shocker, as I would call it. I had been back to work full throttle after the Christmas break and had been catching up on emails, new year meetings and everything else on my ever-growing to-do list. I was driving back from London on the busy A3 and all of a sudden I got this pain under my ribs to the right-hand side – a pain like someone was stabbing me. I couldn't breathe and I panicked so much I thought I was going to crash the car. I couldn't even reach my arm out to change gear as that hurt so much too.

I tried to breathe as gently as I could until I eventually came to a layby where I could pull over. I sat there and waited for about ten minutes for the pain to pass thinking, *I hope the baby is OK*. It wasn't a pain where the baby was though, it was much higher; and it was so scary. I felt totally out of control and scared to start the car again. I made the rest of the 20-minute drive home very slowly, and called my mum as soon as I got in. It's what I always do whenever I am in a flat spin about something: call Mum, *She'll know what to do*.

I always feel so lucky that I can do that, and that she does indeed always know what to do.

The next morning, on Mum's advice, I went to the doctors. She took my blood pressure and chatted to me about what had happened. My blood pressure had gone from fairly low to high in the two weeks since I'd had my last appointment with the midwife. The doctor seemed quite worried about the pain I had experienced. She thought it might have been my gallbladder (which apparently is quite common in pregnancy, who knew?) or a trapped nerve. Either way, she advised me not to drive and signed me off work for the rest of that week and the following one.

I felt a mixture of utter panic and total relief. Panic that I would have to clear my diary and let people down, and relief that someone, an actual professional, had given me permission to slow down; to stop even. Stopping isn't something I am inherently good at – I had been hurtling along in my pregnancy, feeling good and working as hard as I had always done. This was my body telling me to give it a break, so I had to listen. I couldn't believe I had managed to burn out after two weeks back at work! I took the doctor's advice, and stopped.

Those two weeks at home were what I needed. I spent

some time reading and buying some bits and pieces online for the baby. I wanted to rest, but use the time to actually feel like I was starting to get myself organised for the baby's arrival, something I just didn't have the energy to do during weekends between working weeks. We had builders in the house as we had not long started a project upstairs to move the bathroom and guest room and create a nursery. The dust, noise and their insistence on leaving the front door ajar and on the latch (in bloody January, I might add!) was not conducive to relaxation. I spent my days either shut in the sitting room with the log burner roaring or with my mum, who visited to keep me company and bring me lunch.

When I returned to the doctor she signed me off for another week as my blood pressure was still high and she still hadn't managed to get the results of my gall-bladder scan. I was 24 weeks' pregnant, and in those past two weeks I had gone from feeling fabulous to wondering what on earth my body was up to. The main thing remained that the baby was fine and that put my mind at rest hugely.

When I returned to work, it was the second week of February. The doctor had deciphered that the pain had come from a trapped nerve and that I was to limit my driving to no more than one-hour journeys at a time and no more than two or three hours a day in total. I hadn't the heart to tell her that was virtually impossible in my job and that I may as well just quit now. Instead I called my boss and explained my situation. She was really kind and understanding; I think she could hear in my voice that I genuinely wanted to do as much as I could and stay at work for as long as I could. We agreed to cut back my number of meetings in the days and I agreed to get the train as much as I could instead of driving – to me that meant I could use the time to get work done at my laptop rather than wasting time stuck in traffic jams. I also agreed to bring my maternity leave forward, so my last day at work would be at the end of March. I had less than six weeks left at work!

The time hurtled by and before I knew it I was sitting in that last meeting, surrounded by the smiling faces of my wonderful team and being given the most beautiful gifts as my send-off. As I drove out of Hammersmith that day with a boot full of goodies, staring down the barrel of a whole year off work, I felt absolutely elated at the prospect of becoming a mother. I was so ready; ready to start this new chapter of my life. I had loved my career so much and it had always been the centre of my universe. It was so much more important to me than any of my friends' jobs had seemed to them – I cared so much. This felt so strange, that I was excited that I wouldn't be doing it. Becoming a mum felt like my destiny and I couldn't wait.

✦

My first official day of maternity leave involved a lot of pottering around. In fact, I think I spent the next six weeks pottering until I gave birth. I walked Boris every day, as I lived in fear of becoming one of those virtually immobile heavily pregnant women. The work upstairs had just been completed, so I had completely erratic bursts of cleaning around the house – more nesting, I believe – clearing out kitchen cupboards and cleaning the inside of the fridge.

I also celebrated my birthday; Nico and I visited a beautiful spa in the New Forest. I was 36 weeks' pregnant and felt fit to burst (literally, this time). It was supposed to be the last time we did anything 'just us two', and I tried to mentally capture each moment so that I might remember it on the days when I had a restless, screaming baby and take myself back to a place of pure bliss.

A couple of days after my birthday, my brother

Ed got married. It was a wonderful family occasion, when we saw people we hadn't seen for some time and everyone was beaming ear to ear. I was lucky enough to do a reading in the church during the ceremony – 'The Life That I Have' by Leo Marks. I waddled up to the lectern and spoke as well as I could, given the emotion of the day and my raging hormones. I looked at my husband as I read many of those words, but now when I read them it makes me think so strongly of Teddy, too. At the end of that day, as we returned home to my parents' house, I thought, *This was the last thing.* It was the final hurdle I had to get over being pregnant, and I was more than happy for the baby to come any time now.

Naturally those last few weeks of being pregnant dragged. I started to feel as though I had been pregnant for a lifetime. In the latter stages of pregnancy, any woman will tell you that the last thing you want to hear are remarks such as 'Wow aren't you big' (or small – works both ways!) or 'Are you sure you haven't got two in there?' Yes, quite sure, thank you. All of these remarks seem to come thicker and faster, culminating in a feeling that you have indeed been pregnant forever.

The one thing that saved me was yoga. I had gone along with a friend for an evening pregnancy yoga class during my last month at work, and after the first class I was hooked. I was so annoyed at myself that I hadn't discovered it sooner. So, I upped my game during the last six weeks of my pregnancy and went twice a week to make up for lost time. I also practised the breathing techniques at home as a path to relaxation and mindfulness. We hadn't been to NCT or any baby groups, as the NCT course we had booked had been cancelled due to lack of numbers, and by the time they let us know, all of the other courses locally were booked up.

Yoga became my one source of connecting with other women whose babies were due around the same time. It was a way to engage in pregnancy chat, without it being with one of your friends or a well-meaning family member who had already 'been there and done that'. We were all on the same page – a heavily pregnant page in the book of life. Yoga also taught me the breathing exercises and physical moves and stretches that I went on to use during labour. I will be the first to admit that I was one of those awfully sceptical people who thought it was all a load of hot air. Oh, how wrong I was.

Chapter 3

Becoming a Mother

THE WEEKEND THAT TEDDY WAS ON HIS WAY, I KNEW. I HAD FELT PRETTY RESTLESS THAT WEEK. My aunty from America was staying as she had been visiting for my brother's wedding, and I was convinced that my body knew it had to deliver this baby before she went home the following week.

On Friday, 13th May 2016, I had my final appointment with the obstetrician. It was the usual experience at our local hospital of being made to wait for a further two hours or so after your scheduled appointment time, and by the end I felt so exhausted and disenchanted with the whole pregnancy experience. I had loved it, but I was over it. I came home, went on an evening walk with Boris and then proceeded to cook a curry. Like many pregnant women, I had resorted to the school of 'let's try anything' to get this baby moving. Needless to say, as someone who rarely eats spicy food, this wasn't my greatest moment, and it resulted in a night spent on the toilet. My delicate, heavily pregnant constitution just couldn't take this kind of treatment and chose to punish me accordingly. So now I was just overtired and dehydrated to kick off the weekend. Brilliant.

Due to my master plan backfiring (literally), we cancelled the one pregnancy and birth (hospital-organised) crash course day that we had booked in for that Saturday and chose to spend the day quietly at home while I recovered. Sipping on my chilled-down raspberry leaf tea as I watched my husband mow the lawn that afternoon, I knew it wasn't long. Some people say they had no clue, but I did. About six weeks previously I'd woken from a dream, sat bolt upright in bed and said to Nico, 'This baby is going to be born on 16th May,' and then proceeded to go back to sleep. Weird? Yes, totally.

On the Sunday morning, I felt much better. False alarm, this baby was staying put after all. Then as I stood up to go to the bathroom I felt a trickling down my leg. *Great*, I thought, *I have finally lost all control. I am actually pissing myself.* It wasn't coming from *there* though, was it?

Again, I called my mum: 'What does this even mean?'

She told me to ring the delivery suite and just let them know, so I did. They asked me to make my way into the hospital as soon as I could as they thought my waters could be 'leaking'.

Leaking? Bloody leaking? Typical – only I could manage that. There I was hoping for the waters to come crashing out like a movie scene as we are all led to believe will happen, but no. Mine had chosen to *leak*. Apparently this is also incredibly common too. Should have tried harder to re-book those NCT classes elsewhere, shouldn't I?

We made our way to the hospital by 11am. (Turns out I go into full-on faff mode when there's a prospect I might actually have to have a baby that day.) After a quick check over by a midwife, I was rigged up to a monitor for the baby and left to wait it out for a senior midwife to return to inspect the situation in full. About an hour or so passed and they returned as a duo, speculum in hand. A quick sweep around 'in there' confirmed that my back waters (who knew, front and back?) were indeed leaking. The midwife explained that this posed a risk to the baby because of the greater risk of infection. She expected that the obstetrician on duty would want me to be induced that day, but I had to wait for the obstetrician to come and see me to confirm.

We waited a further five hours (it was a Sunday), rigged up to the monitor, wondering if our long-awaited baby would be joining us anytime soon. When the obstetrician came to see me at about 5:30pm she confirmed that they would start the induction process that evening. Thankfully, she was an utterly lovely lady and said that we could nip home first for a shower, dinner and to grab our bags, so that we felt a little more prepared for what was about to happen. Honestly, I don't think anyone really feels prepared when it's the first time, do they?

We did as we were told, made arrangements with friends for them to have Boris, and we were back at the hospital by 9:30pm. As we drove down the slip road towards the hospital I thought to myself that the next time we drove out there would be a little person sitting in that baby seat too. We felt dizzy with excitement.

Once we arrived in the maternity wing, my excitement soon wavered, as it was obvious this was going to be somewhat of a waiting game. We were checked in and shown to the cubicle on the ward where we would be overnight. After some more monitoring and a shift changeover of midwives, the induction process was started with some pessary tablets. I think I had geared myself up for a very dramatic process – let's just say that it didn't live up to that. One midwife popping a few tablets 'up there' didn't exactly have the effect I would have hoped for. I felt pretty normal, and after a few hours a bit crampy.

We made our way through the night with little sleep. I experienced increased tightening around my tummy and I was sure it wouldn't be long until we were in full swing. As the tightening continued and my patience continued to wear thin, I bounced on a birthing ball in the corner of the ward, waiting for our turn to be taken to the delivery suite. Apparently, it's not good news if your baby is coming into the world on a 'busy day' in the UK, as it means there simply isn't space for you to give birth. We had to sit it out and wait for our turn. At midday our time had come, and we followed a midwife down to the delivery suite. By that time I would have been happy to give birth in a corridor.

After about 15 minutes a senior sister appeared and announced she was here to break my front waters (there we go again, back and front!). After I lay flat on the bed with nothing from the waist down and my legs in a rather unflattering fashion, she came at me with what can only be described as a *huge* crochet needle. She then proceeded to rummage around in there (fairly painfully, I might add) until there was a big gush, a huge relief, and I lay there in a warm puddle feeling as though I had wet myself. All of the glamour.

She was on her way out the door to let the other midwife know that the job had been a success, when I stopped her and asked, 'Can I get up now?' to which she replied, 'Well you can if you'd really like. Most people don't like to get up straight away.' All I would like to know is this: who are those people that she speaks of? Lying there, in that puddle of warm 'stuff' (we'll call it that) was one of the single most unpleasant feelings I could recall. I was up, dried off, bed changed and into a fresh nightie before she was back in the room.

It was about quarter to one, and after the waters had been broken I suppose I was in what they would call active labour. The tightenings became deeper contractions after about 20 minutes, and before long I was puffing on that gas and air like nobody's business. I had taken much of the advice that my yoga teacher had given me and chosen to remain standing up for the most part. I was rotating my hips like my life depended on it and trying to use a mixture of deep breaths and the force of gravity to get this baby out. After a few hours like that my legs were running out of steam and I really needed a rest, but I didn't want to lie on the bed, it didn't feel right for me. The midwives were brilliant and put me on what I can only describe as a mini crash mat on the floor. My knees were on the floor and they lowered the bed right down so I could rest my upper body and arms out flat to get some rest.

I think it was at about five o'clock, when I had been trying to push for a while, and was sure that the head was at least trying to make its way out in some capacity, that the midwife leaned around to me and said, 'I can just about see the top of baby's head now.'

What?! I was crestfallen, and utterly exhausted. Surely not? In my mind that moment had passed about an hour ago. Come to think of it, it did seem strange that they hadn't chosen to mention it to me.

After another 45 minutes or so the head was out (not easily I might add, I was flagging). They asked me if I wanted to 'touch babies head' to which I replied something to the tune of, 'Let's not, and say we did.' I think I just wanted it over with, I didn't want to pause for anything. I knew I had to try and reserve my energy for those last few big pushes, but I did just want it finished.

As I leant over the bed, I held on to my husband's hands as he sat across from me – away from the business end of things – and we just looked into each other's eyes. I think he was trying to will me to carry on, to carry me through it with his positive energy; like all men in that position, there was simply nothing he could do. Just before the final push I lifted my head up from the bed, from my pure exhaustion and delirium, and looked at him. Tears rolled down my cheeks, as I simply said, 'Help me.' Of course he couldn't and, with that, I gave it my all, for one last moment.

Oh, the release – the overwhelming physical release and relief of pressure in your body when your baby is born. My shaking knees finally gave in and I collapsed to the floor as the midwife caught Teddy and prevented him from flying out onto the crash mat. She passed him around to me and shifted his umbilical cord out of the way, so I could say to Nico: 'A *boy*. It's a boy.'

See, I knew it.

Chapter 4

Then There Were Three...

MY ELATION QUICKLY TURNED TO THINKING SOMETHING WASN'T QUITE RIGHT. As I crouched there, still on all fours, and holding the baby with the help of the midwife, I realised he was quiet, and floppy. I could sense the panic amongst the three midwives in the room as they hurriedly asked Nico, 'Dad, would you like to cut the cord?' With that, our baby was whisked away, out of the door.

Before I could even ask what was happening, the senior midwife who had been there for the last moments of the birth said, 'Not to worry, it happens all the time. Baby just needs a bit of help, and we'll have him back to you in no time.' I suppose I had watched enough

One Born Every Minute to understand that was quite often the case, but I felt so uneasy. I wanted to hold my baby and I didn't know what was going on.

After a few minutes, Nico was asked if he wanted to join the midwives and consultants with the baby and I was left to deliver the placenta with the assistance of the other midwife. They don't really tell you much about that part, do they? Best kept secrets and all that! I mean, we all *know* that there's a placenta in there too; I supposed I just didn't think much as to its whereabouts and how it might also be making its arrival into this world. It also turned out that mine was a stubborn bastard which, despite an injection and a fair bit of 'tugging' from the encouraging midwife (that actually still makes me shudder a little to think of), wasn't budging. Great. The last resort was me waddling to the bathroom (about ten minutes after having given birth I might add, I am basically a superhero) and sitting on the loo until that thing kind of slid out as I tried to take a pee. (Sorry, Dad, if you are reading this, but that is just Mother Nature.) The image of the placenta might actually haunt me forever – I swear it was bigger than the baby! No wonder I had felt so huge and heavy, it was like having another human in there.

Placenta done and dusted, the midwife was just doing some stitches when the door opened and in came Nico, followed by a smiling lady consultant holding our son wrapped up in a bundle of hospital towels and wearing what can only be described as a blue fisherman's hat. I do love that the NHS supply those little knitted hats for all of the newborns, but his made him look like he was about to head off on a deep-sea excursion and had a penchant for whisky drinking.

My relief at seeing him was palpable. I knew everyone in the room could feel it. The smile on my husband's face was one I had never seen before – utter pride and sheer joy. The consultant explained to us that baby had had a little trouble 'getting going' as it were, and it had meant that he needed a rub down with a towel and an oxygen mask to get him breathing. He was now breathing and stable as far as she was concerned, and had scored well on the newborn tests. She handed him to me and told me to get some skin-to-skin time with him. Cue me whipping my top down as quickly as I could (knees still firmly up in the air as the midwife finished the job down there); I couldn't wait to have him back, to hold him for the first time, properly.

As I lay there, beaming, and studying every detail of his little face, Nico called our parents and told them the happy news. It was early evening when he had been born, so our parents had been waiting all day for the phone to ring. My parents had been at our house, looking after Boris and waiting to head over to meet their new grandchild as soon as possible, but by the time we called them it was gone 7pm and we agreed that they would head home, taking Boris with them. They'd come to the hospital in the morning when we were all a little less hazy and had had some rest. I wanted us to spend some hours with our son, in this little bubble, just us three. It felt so surreal – when I think back now, it's like an out of body experience, like it happened to someone else, but I think our memory has a tendency to do that to us sometimes, doesn't it? Makes it feel like a dream.

One thing I had noticed about our baby boy was that he wasn't crying yet. He also hadn't opened his eyes, and I was dying to see them. As far as I was concerned he was basically a carbon copy of Nico, so I was expecting to see those twinkly blue eyes when he eventually opened them. When the midwife came in to try and help me to help him feed for the first time, there was a brief moment when he yawned and his eyes semi-opened. They were sort of rolled up in his lids and I couldn't make them out properly, but all

I could see was crystal blue. I said to Nico, 'His eyes are definitely yours too.' I tried to feed him, but he seemed sleepy and disinterested. The midwife said that she suspected that it was because he was very drowsy and needed to sleep; as did we. She suggested that we begin to get our things together to be moved down to the ward for the night.

Before we did, I took the opportunity to speak to my mum on a video call; I was desperate for her to see him and see me. I think I wanted her to know that we were both OK, as I had been so worried about giving birth and wanted her to see I had got through it. She cooed over the unexpectedly tiny baby I was still clutching to my chest and I showed her his perfect little heart-shaped face. She was as happy and as proud as I was expecting her to be, and we both just kept smiling and then crying all of the happy tears.

We changed him into a tiny one-piece suit and a new hat (the fisherman-chic still wasn't doing anything for him). I remember feeling like the most ill-prepared mother ever as I didn't have the right nappies for him. He was so tiny that the newborn ones I had brought with us were huge on him, but luckily the student midwife came to the rescue with some 'tiny baby' nappies, as she called them. He certainly was tiny.

Wheeling him down the corridor to the ward, I felt so proud. I wanted to stop every single person who passed me in the corridor – doctor, midwife, innocent passer-by, I didn't care – to show everyone our son and say, 'Look what we made!' I don't think I have ever felt so beaming with pride about anything in my life, and I certainly haven't since.

We made it to the ward, despite my snail's pace, and found ourselves in a ward of other parents whose babies had needed a little extra care at birth, or whose births had been more difficult than anticipated. It meant that all of the babies (and mums) in there would be checked more frequently through the night and that I would get a good night's sleep knowing that baby was being watched and looked after.

You'll notice that I haven't given the baby a name yet. We had it down to a shortlist of two, and were still deciding even in the hours after he was born. I wanted to get to know him, to see what suited him and feel like I knew him before he got a name. The tag around his ankle said 'Baby Wright', but by the time we had walked him to the ward, we knew he was our Teddy. So, we tucked him up in his cot and tried to get some sleep. I thought how peaceful he looked, so angelic, so perfect.

Chapter 5

Just 74 Hours on this Earth

I FELT LIKE I HAD ONLY JUST BEGUN TO DRIFT OFF WHEN THE MIDWIFE ON DUTY RETURNED AND WOKE US. She said that Teddy was a little cold and could probably do with a cuddle. I remember her saying that she would make a note of it, but that it was nothing to worry too much about. Babies have trouble regulating their own temperature after they are born, so again it's not uncommon for them to be cold. Of course I obliged and picked him straight up for a cuddle. She suggested I maybe try to get him to feed again, but he still wasn't interested; his eyes firmly closed, he just wanted to sleep. After 15 minutes or so she came back and asked me if he felt any warmer; he did to us, but she checked him over and then said we could put him back in his cot. I tucked him up once more and gave him a kiss.

The next thing that happened can only be described as a living nightmare. The midwife woke me again; I had no idea what time it was. How much time had passed since the last wake up? She shook my shoulder so hard and said, 'I'm going to take him now, he's really cold. I have to take him.' Nico and I sat bolt upright in bed, just as she disappeared with Teddy. As she lifted him I remember clearly seeing his little arms flop down by his side, lifeless. Something was really wrong this time. I could see shadows of people sprinting down the corridors past the ward, a panic light was flashing. Another midwife returned to our cubicle and hastily pulled the curtains around to protect us from what was unfolding outside the ward. I could hear it though; I knew it was bad. As she sat with us she just kept rubbing my arm and squeezing my hand and repeating, 'It's OK, he'll be OK. He's in the best place with the doctors. They'll look after him for you.' I wanted to scream and run out of that cubicle and down the corridor and find my son. I wanted him back.

We must have been sat with her for about 20 minutes, every second of which feeling as though it lasted a lifetime, before a senior midwife decided to move us to another room. It wasn't a room with a bed, just a waiting room with chairs around the outside, and she ushered me into one of the plastic chairs. I was still in my pyjamas, barefoot and barely recovered from giving birth. I had no clue what the hell was going on, or what we were about to be told.

After some time, a consultant walked in and introduced himself to us. He crouched down in front of our chairs to speak to us, ashen faced and looking as though he was searching for the right words to start his sentence. Before he uttered a single word, I knew our lives had just changed forever – the expression on his face said everything.

The words, 'You have a very sick little boy,' will stay with me forever. He explained that he and his team had struggled to bring Teddy back, that he had been resuscitated for over 18 minutes. For 18 minutes they had put that little body through hell, trying to spark it back to life. He couldn't tell us how long Teddy hadn't been breathing before the midwife had found him; they didn't know. I just remember feeling so thankful that they had brought him back, that he was still here.

The consultant said that Teddy was in their SCBU (Special Care Baby Unit) for now, being stabilised and monitored, but that they didn't have the specialist facilities to care for him. He would need to be transferred to a nearby hospital and to a NICU (Neonatal Intensive Care Unit) as soon as possible. Luckily, at that moment I knew not what SCBU nor NICU meant, they were just acronyms to me, just sounds. Had I understood either, I would have understood the severity of Teddy's situation, and of ours. I was in a haze of shock, tiredness and hormones; I barely knew which way was up. I wasn't in a position to understand any of it. It was already gone 2:30am, so the midwives took us to a private room where we tried to get a few hours' sleep until the morning. Miraculously, I think through pure exhaustion, we did and were woken just before 7am.

Two midwives came in to check on us and give us as much of an update as they could. They explained that we would most likely be able to go and visit Teddy in the SCBU before they transferred him to the other hospital. They were just waiting to hear confirmation of whether they had room for him in a neighbouring Surrey hospital or whether he would be transferred to St George's in London.

They asked if we wanted breakfast and tried to encourage us both to eat. Unsurprisingly I wasn't hungry, but I did want to eat. I felt like I hadn't eaten in days, which was true – it was Tuesday morning and I hadn't had an actual meal since Sunday night. NHS food wasn't really calling out to me, so I sent Nico down to the M&S in the hospital to pick some food up for the both of us. I called my parents to tell them not to set off for the hospital to see us this morning, and explained what had happened to Teddy in the night.

When I think back now, I completely downplayed the severity of what was happening. I didn't want to worry my parents; I kept saying that he was OK and just being transferred to another hospital to be better looked after. I didn't tell them about the length of time he had been resuscitated or that he was currently on a ventilator. I told my mum we would call later, once we knew which hospital we were transferring to, and that we would love for them to come later that day. I needed a hug from my parents as much as anything. Nico called his parents, too. I couldn't believe we were having to do this; one minute we had been delivering the happiest of news to them all, and now this.

Later that morning we were allowed in to see Teddy. As we were led along the corridor by a very nervous-looking senior midwife, I got a further sense of how bad things really were. They kept telling us to be prepared to be shocked when we saw him, but nothing could have prepared me for what we walked in to. A small room of babies in what looked to me like big plastic fish tanks; my eyes darted so quickly around the room as I looked for my baby. He was in the corner, in the biggest tank, with the most equipment around him, two doctors monitoring him. The beeping and bleeping from the machines was deafening, and he looked so tiny – tinier than ever in that tank. Covered by wires and only wearing a nappy; still so fresh into this world and yet already fighting for his life. Hot, heavy tears poured down my cheeks as I stared in at him. I didn't realise I wouldn't be able to touch him, that I had to stare in at my son on the other side of that tank. Completely helpless, both of us. Nico squeezed my hand and kept telling me it would be OK, that the doctors were looking after him. I knew they were, but my instinct was telling me that I just wanted my baby in my arms.

A little while later we got confirmation that it would be the hospital near Chertsey in Surrey that Teddy would be transferred to. I know it sounds like such a trivial thing to be relieved about, but knowing that we wouldn't be transferred into London was such a relief.

On top of everything, I didn't want our families to be making that trip in to meet Teddy, especially given the circumstances. The ambulance was nearly ready to transfer him, and I waited to be discharged by the midwives, filling in all of the relevant paperwork.

I should have known it was the worst news when she said, 'We won't give you a red book for him. I am sure that St Peter's can give you that when you get there.' In other words, your baby won't need a red book, he isn't coming home. I didn't know that then though – the truth is I didn't even know what the red book was. I was a first-time mum and completely clueless as to what I was supposed to expect.

The midwives were so kind, they kept reassuring us and they hugged us goodbye as we left the ward. When I think back to it now it seems utterly bizarre. There I was, some 14 hours after having given birth for the first time, now being discharged and waved off out of the hospital by the midwives when my baby was leaving in a specialist ambulance. Yet it all seemed so calm. Had I really, and I mean *really*, sensed what was going on, I would have been screaming and crying, barely able to walk myself out of there, but I didn't, I just smiled and thanked them and we went on our way, without our newborn son.

The thing for me that really stands out in my mind as to just how clueless we were as to what was coming next: before we drove to the new hospital, we came home. Yes, we didn't realise that our son was actually dying and never going to come home with us, and so we came back to our house. I wanted to have a shower, not in a hospital, at home. My husband wanted to do the same, and we both packed some fresh clothes. Of course, I was bleeding and leaking and by all rights should barely have been bloody well walking, let alone popping home for a quick shower. I was in agony, and Nico had to help me wash and dress, and repack my bag for me.

I still had Teddy's baby-bag packed for him; oh, how I had packed that little hospital bag so neatly and with such great anticipation for what lay ahead. Even when we went home I didn't think not to bring it again, I very nearly added more of the things I thought he would need.

Looking back, this all sounds utterly crazy; we even popped keys over to our neighbour to ask her to feed the cat when we were at the hospital. We were only at home for less than an hour, but the guilt I have now for not going straight to the hospital to spend every waking second with Teddy.

We arrived at the NICU at lunchtime. We were given the name of the building and ward we needed to go to by the midwives at our hospital. It all felt so surreal, walking into an entirely new hospital, where neither of us had ever been before. We took the lift to the floor signposted Neonatal Intensive Care Unit, and then it hit me like a lightning bolt. *'Intensive Care' – that's what NICU means?* This was really bad. I knew my parents would be with us in a matter of hours and I just kept telling myself that all would be well once they were there.

We buzzed the door and they let us in. The lady at reception seemed to know who we were before either of us opened our mouths. Perhaps it was the look on our faces – slightly grey from tiredness and shock, looking like we didn't know what day of the week it was.

'Mr and Mrs Wright? You've come from Royal Surrey?' she said. 'I'll just get a consultant for you. Take a seat. Teddy is here and he is just being settled in Nursery One.'

Nursery One? She made it sound so lovely, like he was there for a little holiday. Double doors led to the area where everything was happening; she disappeared through them and we waited.

The truth is, and I am sure this is to do with a vicious

cocktail of shock and hormones, I remember very little detail of what happened for the remainder of that day. This is what I do recall: being moved down to a room in the maternity ward for a couple of hours before we could see Teddy, where lots of kind midwives came to see us, and again tried to get me to eat something. I remember being continually asked if I needed any pain relief, or if I needed anything. I felt like saying, 'I need this to stop. I need to get my son and go home. I need this nightmare to be over.' Of course, we just smiled politely and cried when they weren't there.

After some time we were able to move our things back up to the floor where the NICU was; they said we would have a room we could stay in up there. The room was a huge hospital suite with a bed, sofas and its own bathroom. It felt less like a hospital room, which was nice. I know now that's because it was a bereavement suite. A quiet corner away from the noise of newborn cries in the main delivery rooms; somewhere that women who were delivering their stillborn babies could do so away from it all. Not all hospitals have one, but they should; they *really should*.

We were finally allowed to see Teddy. We were greeted by a lady consultant, who said she was looking after our baby. 'Wow, big parents. I wasn't expecting to see such big parents.' Luckily I am not easily offended, and knew she wasn't referring to the extra bit of timber I had acquired during pregnancy – my husband and I are both tall. Teddy had weighed in at just 6lb 2oz when he was born and to me he looked *so* tiny. I had tipped the scales at 9lb 8oz at birth, so I had been expecting a whopper. He wasn't; just tiny little Teddy, small and perfectly formed.

The consultant had said exactly what I had been thinking – why was our baby, born just a few days before his due date, so small? She said he wasn't tiny, but that she would have expected a bigger baby from big, healthy parents. I immediately sensed that she was one of the most intuitive and intellectual people I had ever met. It was almost as though she was already sensing what was wrong with Teddy and she needed to get to the bottom of it.

Again, she warned us that it wouldn't be nice seeing him in the nursery as he was rigged up to lots of machines; but we didn't care, we needed to see him. Much to my relief, Teddy was one of the only babies in the room who wasn't in a 'fish tank', he was back in what looked like the same plastic crib he had been in the night before in the maternity unit, just a little bigger. Of course, I know now that the kind of incubator he was in is very specialist and hugely expensive, and was in fact one of the reasons we were waiting on whether he could be treated in that NICU. They only had space and equipment to treat one 'sick' baby like Teddy. The rest of the unit was set up to treat premature babies born earlier than their due dates, but Teddy was there for very different reasons and the equipment that surrounded him suggested that. I didn't care, his crib wasn't closed in and I wanted to touch him, to stroke his face and hold his hand.

'Wait, before you touch him. I just want you to know that he is cold.'

Cold, still? How can he be?

The consultant told us that Teddy had been put onto a specialist cooling mat, used often to treat babies who have been starved of oxygen and are at risk of brain damage. It is proven that by cooling the body they can lessen the extent of the damage and give that child a better chance of recovery.

'Brain damage? What do you mean?' I asked.

She explained that Teddy had been revived for 18 minutes and also repeated what the consultant at the other hospital had told us, that they didn't know how long before he had been found that he hadn't been breathing. Essentially, his brain had been starved of oxygen for a huge amount of time. He had wires attached to his little fuzzy blond head; these were monitoring his brain activity, she explained. The lines on the screen were flat, with an intermittent flicker.

My heart sank, I felt a burning in my throat as I gulped and those hot tears burned down my face once more. We were able to see him for a little while before she took as to a quiet room for a chat about how they would proceed. She explained that they planned to run tests on Teddy; blood tests, urine tests and other scans, including an MRI scan the following day, where he would be taken to the other side of the hospital. I remember her assuring us that they were doing everything they could for Teddy, and that he was comfortable – he was heavily sedated and wasn't in any pain.

I believed that he was in the right place and that they were moving mountains to help him, and I hoped that he couldn't feel any pain at all. My instinct as a mother was to sweep him up into my arms and hold him closely, feeling I could make it all better; but the truth is I wasn't allowed to even hold him. My heart actually ached to do so.

Not long after our meeting with the consultant, both of our parents arrived. I just remember crying into my mum's shoulder and her letting me do so. I wanted her to tell me that it would all be better, that she would make sure of it, like she had been able to with so many other situations in my life to date. There was nothing anyone could do, we all knew that.

Only two people at a time were able to sit with Teddy next to his crib, so we took it in turns; both sets of his grandparents and Nico's sister, Zoe, and her husband, sat with him that day. Everyone wanted to meet him. I remember Mum saying how perfect he was, how he looked like a little cherub, and how soft the back of his little neck was. All things I had thought too.

That evening, after everyone had gone home, we sat with Teddy and we talked to him. I began to learn what each machine did and watched those monitors. I willed him to open his eyes, to wake up and to be well enough for us to pick him up and come home. I told him about everything that was waiting for him in his nursery, all of the things we had lovingly collected for him in those nine months, and how I couldn't wait for him to see it. I am pretty sure that Nico and I both used up every single wish we both ever had in those moments. We wished for this to be better and for

Teddy to come home. I felt us both willing him back to life. If I could have breathed the life back into him, I would have, but the feeling of helplessness continued.

The next day became a similar repetition of tests and scans, and another meeting with the consultant and NICU nurses. The consultant caring for Teddy said that once he had had an MRI scan she would send the results to another professor at Great Ormond Street, with whom she had already been discussing Teddy's current condition. I felt so sure that she was going to get to the bottom of why Teddy was so poorly. I can remember us both thanking her and she even said to us, 'I am going to try my hardest to find out why your son is so poorly. I promise you that.' Knowing that so many people were rooting for Teddy was keeping us going.

A few of our friends now knew our situation and were sending messages of support, letting us know they were thinking of Teddy and sending positive vibes to us. Being in that hospital was like being in a bubble, so it was nice to know that people were out there and knew about Teddy. Friends sent photos to us of candles that they had lit for Teddy. I exchanged a couple of messages with my very closest friends, but I couldn't face speaking to anyone on the phone or returning everyone's messages. It was too overwhelming. I didn't take my phone into the room Teddy was in anyway, so I barely had it with me. We weren't even allowed to wear watches or jewellery there because of the risk of infection, so everything stayed in our room.

Later that day Teddy went for his MRI scan in another giant fish tank – we waved him off down the corridor as the hospital transportation team and his nurse from the unit went with him. I put his little fluffy penguin in with him too, a gift from our niece who was just two at the time; I didn't want him to get lonely on his travels. I kept the toy elephant from his hospital crib with me as I counted down the seconds to his return. Once he did return, we spent the rest of that afternoon and evening with him, and for the first time since his birth we were able to hold him again. It wasn't an easy thing to organise due to all of his wires and associated hardware, but we did manage to have him on our laps, on his cooling mat. It was a strange experience and not how any mother envisages holding her newborn, but it was a memory I will cherish, as it was one of the few normal things we had been able to do as his parents. That evening we read him books over his crib until it was late and I could barely keep my eyes open. It was probably after midnight before the nurses finally persuaded us to go to bed and that he was safe with them, but I didn't want to leave – it was almost as though I had a sixth sense that would be the last evening we spent with Teddy.

★

The next day started as the previous had done. A breakfast I avoided, more painkillers from the midwives and a shower that hurt like hell in my nether regions. We waited for our morning get-together with the consultant to discuss the latest on Teddy's progress, or rather, as we were coming to learn, lack of it.

That day was also the day my milk came in – yay. As someone who has been virtually flat-chested my entire adult life, never had there been a time that I had been less likely to be enthusiastic about my new Katie Price (c. 2003) breasts. I even lifted my top up to show my husband that morning and said the words, 'Well, these couldn't have come at a worse time!' Luckily, we both still had our sense of humour. I think we are very much of the school of 'if you don't laugh, you'll cry', and we had both done so much crying over those few days, we needed to laugh at something. My inappropriately timed norks became the joke that kept on giving.

When we went in to see the consultant that morning,

she said she was just waiting to hear back from the professor at Great Ormond Street. All of the tests that they had run on Teddy so far had shown nothing. She said she had had a feeling it was perhaps something wrong with his metabolic system, but she didn't have test results for that yet, and that those results could take up to eight weeks to come back to her. Of course, we knew we didn't have eight weeks to wait; Teddy was deteriorating by the day. I just wanted the MRI scan to bring us some good news, that there was something there, a flicker of hope.

Nico's parents came to spend some time with us, and just after they left, my parents arrived. Those hours were a blur of us making chit-chat and all trying to spend as much time in with Teddy as we could.

Not long after my parents arrived, the time came to see the consultant again. We knew this would be the meeting at which they told us the outcome for Teddy and I asked if my mum and dad could come in with us. More and more people seemed to be coming into the room to take a seat for this chat – our consultant, the registrars who had cared for Teddy, the senior NICU nurse, the nurse who was caring for Teddy most of the time and the senior paediatric consultant. I knew things had reached their tipping point, and we'd be moving from this bubble of our current reality to a new one that I couldn't quite bare to think about.

I watched and listened as the senior consultant began to speak about Teddy, the rest of the room so silent you could hear a pin drop. The bright May sunshine of the past few days had turned to grey clouds and rain outside the vast windows that were beside us. I felt sick as I listened. We found out there was nothing they could do for Teddy and that he would die that day.

I don't think I could ever describe how that felt. Believe me, I have tried to many times since, but it's a truly inexplicable feeling, one I wouldn't wish upon anyone. All I can say is this – I felt as though every last breath had been kicked out of my chest, as if a wave had pulled me under and no matter how hard I kicked, screamed or struggled, I was never coming up for air. The feeling engulfed me.

Now that this had happened, I knew it was totally irreversible; that our lives, no matter how hard we tried or how much time passed, would never be the same. I wanted to be able to think straight, to talk back to them and ask questions. No one else was speaking from our side of the room; not my husband, nor my parents. I asked the first question that came into my head as my response to the news that Teddy had no brain activity and was deteriorating physically each day. 'Is that damage irreversible?'

'Yes,' came the answer, as he nodded and looked to the floor. I could see tears streaming down the faces of the hospital staff. I saw six people sitting in front of us who wanted, so badly, to tell a desperate, pleading mother who was grasping at the final straws for her son's life that it was OK and that he was going to get better; but they couldn't. I could see how much it hurt them all, and how they wished this wasn't the news they had to deliver either.

We agreed that they would withdraw Teddy's life support that evening. It was already gone 3:30pm. We had a matter of hours with him. As they left the room, I howled out in physical pain and collapsed into my mum's arms. She sobbed into me and held me so tightly. She hugged both Nico and I together and just kept saying sorry, as did I. I watched as my dad stood staring motionless and silently out of the window, tears rolling down his cheeks and an expression of complete disbelief. Nico called his parents and asked them to come back.

★

The hours that led up to our final goodbye with Teddy felt as though they moved in slow motion. We finally got to cuddle him again, skin on skin, out of his tank. His grandparents held him close for the first time. We took our only photos as a family of three. We washed him, changed him and dressed him in a romper suit and hat – he had been in just a nappy for days. I finally felt like a proper mummy, looking after him.

I didn't want him just being 'switched off' in a room full of other babies and their families. No matter how private they made it, it didn't feel right. Instead he was brought to us in a room with our family, and I sat on a sofa flanked by my husband and my mum. As his nurse stopped pumping air into his lungs she removed the final pieces of tape from around his mouth and handed him to us. Finally, he was free from all those wires, all that beeping and buzzing; no more machines, just my perfect boy.

As he took his last gasping breaths we read him a story, *Guess How Much I Love You?*. It was a loaned book from his cousin and I had read it to him in his tank the previous evening when I had hoped it might make him better. I had never read that book before, and I haven't read it since, but those words will stay in my mind forever. I was lost in them as I tried to photographically memorise every last detail of his perfect little face, and the weight of him in my arms.

Then those tiny breaths stopped. At 8:31pm, on Thursday, 19th May 2016, Teddy left us, not in any more pain, for his big party in the sky.

I didn't feel scared when he took his last breaths, because I didn't want him to know that I was scared; I wanted him to feel safe and that his mummy loved him. That's what a mother does, isn't it? Forgets her own feelings in order to protect those of her children. I think I felt my heart physically breaking in that moment; at least, that is all I can describe that feeling as.

As we tucked him back into the hospital cot, we kissed him, stroked his little face, and I breathed in that scent for the last time. I felt as though I was tucking him in, kissing him goodnight, but for the first and very last time all at once. As they wheeled him away I caught one last glimpse of him and his toy elephant next to him, and I knew that would be the final time I laid eyes on him. He looked so perfect, so peaceful. I wanted that as our lasting memory.

Chapter 6

What Now?

LIKE MOST PEOPLE IN THE SHOCK AND AFTERMATH OF
A SUDDEN LOSS; THE WORD 'NUMB' COMES TO MIND.
Numbness; physically and emotionally. I wasn't even
sure which way was up. We had returned home the
night that Teddy had died. The hospital had offered
for us to stay one more night, but we both needed to
get out of there. I had barely slept since Sunday and it
was Thursday. The week had seemed as though it had
run in slow motion, but at the same time it all felt like
a total blur.

All I thought in those first hours, during the journey
home and when we arrived back was, *No, not us.*
Things like this happen to other people. It's like my

mind was actually refusing to believe the outcome. Whether that was a mix of hormones and my body refusing to believe that I didn't have a baby in my arms after nine long months of pregnancy, I shall never know. At a guess, I would say it was the cocktail of shock, grief, sleep deprivation and hormones that contributed to my complete refusal to believe that this had, in fact, just happened to us.

I didn't want to speak to anyone, I couldn't face it. I felt guilty, I felt ashamed even. Other people managed to be pregnant, have a baby and then bring that baby home. Why not me? What had I done *so* wrong? All these questions whirred around in my head at a hundred miles an hour. I couldn't help thinking I had let everyone down; they were expecting the happiest news and I had given them this. I kept telling Nico it was all my fault, that I must have done something wrong in Teddy's pregnancy. I remember saying to everyone, 'I am so sorry,' until my mum banned those words and said she couldn't keep hearing me apologise for something that wasn't my fault. I kept feeling it was though, and that feeling ate away at me.

I sent a few messages to a few friends, just the ones who had known what had been going on since Teddy's arrival. I can't recall my exact words, but

I think I simply explained that we had had to say goodbye to Teddy and that he was just too perfect for this world. That was all I could manage, I couldn't say 'He died' or 'He's dead', I wouldn't allow myself to. I think it took a few months before I could say or write those two words together. 'Teddy died.' For the friends that I told, I made it crystal clear that I needed to be left alone. I didn't want to see anyone, I couldn't face it. I asked one of my closest friends to tell others what had happened. I didn't want to regurgitate the whole sorry tale again and again; I didn't have the strength.

My parents stayed with us, thankfully. We needed the support, and I think they needed us as much as we did them. They made sure we ate and that I rested. The midwives visited over the days that followed. I can remember sitting there in my dressing gown on the end of my bed, howling in physical pain as the first midwife came to see me. I couldn't stop my body from shaking; I felt empty, like a piece of me was gone forever. I don't think anyone can really put into words what it feels like to have a broken heart – I have often wondered if it is even really possible. Those first few days were a physical pain. A loss so deep and shocking, coupled with the physical loss of me no longer being pregnant. That was a broken heart, I was sure of it. It took everything I had to get out of bed in the mornings. I would sit there at the edge of the bed and just wonder, *Why am I doing this?*

I could not see what my purpose was anymore; I felt purposeless. That was what I said to each midwife and that was what I said to Mum each time we spoke about what had happened. My mum kept reassuring me that I wasn't and that I was still Teddy's mummy, whether he was here or not. I cannot imagine how hard those first few hours and days must have been on her, trying to support me as her daughter, watching me howl with cries of pain and not being able to protect me from any of it, all the while as she had just lost her grandson. She showed me so much love and support, for which I don't think I will ever really be able to show my true gratitude.

The first few days felt as though we mainly sat around crying and staring blankly at each other. My brothers and my sisters-in-law came to visit, and Nico's parents were there whenever they could be. As a family we were facing the unthinkable, and were still trying to make chit-chat and sit out in the May sunshine in the garden. I felt as though the weather was taunting me; mocking my life and what had just happened to us. I wanted it to suit my mood and just cloud over, and yet the sun kept shining.

Of course, when we arrived home, we had a house with a nursery, a pram in the hallway and a Moses basket set up in our bedroom. Nico hid everything in the nursery and closed the door. I didn't want to go in there, I couldn't even step foot in that direction of the landing upstairs. Each time I looked down the hallway I could see the cracks of bright light shining through the old oak door, flooding though from that sun-drenched nursery. Those beams of light showing me what was missing from my life on the other side of that door; a life that I had been shut out of.

The rest of my home really was (still is) my sanctuary during those days. Family came and went but I stayed put, too scared to step foot out of the door. I was fearful of the life that would greet me when I did. Scared of telling people, scared of the people who already knew who might cross the road to avoid me. The thought of seeing anyone doing either of those things made me feel sick. It was a little like being a prisoner in your own home – a prison full of flowers that kept arriving.

I know that there is so little people feel they can do in the wake of a tragedy and so they think flowers are the best option. But by the time I had opened the door to the tenth bunch, I hated flowers. (Don't ever tell my husband that I actually said that, as this comes from the woman who readily spends money on fresh flowers for the house every week!) I begged everyone who visited to take some flowers with them; of course, they wouldn't as they felt somehow that they were taking a piece of something that had been given to Teddy.

The cards came in droves too – cards of sympathy, cards filled with outpourings of love from friends and family. Even cards from people I had barely spoken to in recent months and years. It seemed that everyone was finding out and everyone wanted to let us know that they cared. My mobile phone was forever filled with reams of messages from well-meaning friends. I can recall Nico saying, 'Will you just put the phone down, it upsets you even more.' He was right, it did. Reading people's kind and heartfelt words only made it hurt more; made the reality of what had happened start to set in.

My parents left at the beginning of the following week. They had to get back to their own commitments, but we also needed time to digest what had happened. My husband had tried his very best at being 'normal' by still leaving the house to go to the shops, to walk Boris or to go on a run. All of which seemed to result in him returning to the house in tears again and again. My fear of the outside world built up in my head even further.

I had never suffered with anxiety before in my life, but all of that changed the moment that Teddy stopped breathing that first night. Ever since then I existed in a cloud of angst and worry, terrified about what was about to unfold next in our story. After Teddy died those feelings worsened. I think it was because I realised that the unthinkable could and had happened; that anything could indeed happen. In the worst possible way. The intensity of a feeling that something terrible was just around the corner; and then your subconscious suddenly remembering that it had already happened. Anxiety, for me, was cruel and overbearing. It crept into every part of my day and caused me to be scared of even my phone ringing or a knock at the front door. It felt as though the world had become a noisy, terrifying place that I just couldn't face being a part of; I didn't want to face any of it without Teddy, but I knew I would have to.

Other than the visits from the regular midwives, we were also booked an appointment with the bereavement midwife in the days that followed. It was the Wednesday after Teddy had died, just six days had passed, but it was a day that will stay in my mind for so many reasons – a day of realisation, if you like. I'm not entirely sure how long shock lasts when you lose a baby. I am sure it must be very different for everyone. Maybe it was because my hormones were settling down – my engorged breasts had finally turned a corner and my milk production was stopping. I think my body was beginning to understand what had happened; in part, at least.

It was the morning after my parents had left. As I lay in bed, I watched the light creep through the shutters on the window. The window had been open overnight and so I could hear footsteps of people on their way to the train station; commuters and school children leaving for the day ahead. The builder on the roof opposite began to whistle a tune as he retiled the roof of the house, and the sun continued to creep even further through those cracks. No one in that outside world knew, did they? Not one of them had a single clue about how our lives had just been changed forever; unrecognisably changed. That was the moment that I realised, *Life just goes on.* Whether I chose to partake or to remain forever in the safety and security of my home in my dressing gown, and some days I do still feel like just going back to that, it was bloody well going to happen.

That was it, my moment. I got up and I showered.

I put on some clothes that fit (those were few and far between, I can tell you) and I put on my make-up. I looked in the mirror and I saw 'me'. Yes, she looked tired and a little (OK, *a lot*) fatter than usual, but it was still me; I was still in there somewhere.

When the midwife arrived, I greeted her at the door with a smile and asked her if I could get her a cup of tea. I think she thought I was totally mental, as though she should be getting straight on the phone to the hospital and saying to her colleague, 'Yep, Jane, we've got a real problem here. This one isn't even crying and she's dressed. I think she might have even washed her hair. We've got a code red.'

My husband and I sat with her for around an hour, and in that time I quickly realised that speaking to her about Teddy wasn't going to be incredibly useful for me. For starters, she hadn't even bothered to learn Teddy's name before her arrival; to her, he was just a nameless, faceless baby who had never made it home. I can remember thinking, *YOU HAD ONE JOB!* My notes were the size of an ancient tablet by this point as they combined Teddy's notes from the NICU. I just thought she could have at least given them a flick though to find out his name before she stepped into the house and proceeded to try and counsel us.

I went out of my way to show her photographs of him, to show her who he was. I don't think she liked my style, and to be brutally honest I wasn't the biggest fan of hers. My parents have always brought me up to deal with everything head on, to use laughter as a tonic in the face of adversity and to speak your mind. She wanted me to sit and sob, but I had done that for six days. I wasn't just going to sit and turn on the waterworks for her benefit. If she was here to talk to me about our son and what had happened then that was what I was going to do.

It was a little like talking to a human bereavement textbook – she kept pausing at extremely forced moments, and I can only assume these were appropriate moments in which we were supposed to use the time to grieve and/or reflect on just how shit our situation was right now. I told her I had an idea for fundraising as I wanted to help the hospital and her response was, 'Are you sure you are ready?' I think it was the moment that my husband (usually the most easy-going man I know) said, 'Right, are we done here then?' that I knew he was as uncomfortable in her company as I was.

She offered to see us again for a return visit, and we politely declined. I can't say that the hospital didn't try to help us, they did; she just wasn't the right person for us on that day and I felt as though she should have been more sensitive to how we were grieving for our son. Instead she tried to force textbook rules of grieving upon us that had no relevance to how we were feeling on that particular day. After all, we are all different – and we aren't textbooks, we are humans.

That visit was the final straw for us both. The intensity of the week after Teddy's death was getting to us and we felt trapped in the house. We needed to get away. We hadn't seen any friends, but I didn't want to either, for now at least. The funeral was on hold as we were waiting to hear from the coroner's office. Teddy had died in the care of the NHS without an actual diagnosis as to why he had fallen ill, so the coroner was aiming to find answers to our questions. In the meantime, he was trying to issue us with a temporary death certificate that would enable us to go ahead with a funeral and a cremation.

The phone in the house and our mobile phones had felt as though they were ringing off the hook as a result. The hospital, the coroner, the NICU checking we were OK, the bereavement midwife, the doctor's surgery, who had heard about Teddy; everyone cared, but it was all too much to take. Too many phone calls and too many letters about investigations and what was to happen next. I just wanted to deal with one person about the whole thing, but it didn't seem to work like that. Perhaps it will someday, as I think that would be a very worthwhile change for bereaved parents who are living with the immediate shock in the wake of losing a child.

We booked a trip to Cornwall for the end of that week. Just a week after Teddy had died and ten days since his birth and we were booking a bloody mini break. Not how I had seen the first two weeks into our journey as parents going, I must say.

Cornwall had always been our refuge, come rain or shine. I remember saying to Nico, 'I just need to sit on the beach, stare at the sea and make some sense of this.' Of course, there was no sense to be made. What I was thinking, I don't know. My mum booked us a little self-catering cottage, tucked away, where Boris would be welcome too. Boris was a must – he hadn't left my side since we returned home from the NICU. He was one of the few things that had made me smile.

As we drove down to Cornwall the numbness seemed to deepen. I was overwhelmed with the feelings of, *We shouldn't be doing this, this isn't how it was supposed to be.* The journey saw me in tears for most of the way. The cottage was perfect; beautiful in every way. Its own courtyard garden, not overlooked, peaceful and hidden away from the world. Exactly where I needed to be. As much as I had hoped it would be, Cornwall just wasn't the tonic I had hoped for. In the past, it had always been able to solve so many of my worries and problems. This one wasn't that easy. There was no taking away from the pain of what had just happened and we both realised that inevitably quickly after we arrived. It was nice to be away from home in as much as I felt disconnected with the world, as though we had left real life behind, but part of me longed to be back in our home, shut away from the world and feeling protected by the surroundings of my own things.

We tried our very best to do the things we always enjoyed doing when we were down there, but of course it was all too much, too soon. It didn't help that it was the May Day bank holiday and school half-term, so when we visited our favourite beaches we had to face hordes of families, rather than the quiet bays we were used to. I remember sitting on the beach at Harlyn Bay, one of our favourite places just along the coastal path from my parents-in-law's house. I had last been there at New Year, when I was pregnant with Teddy. In my mind, he had already been to that beach, and the next time we were to visit he'd be on the outside instead of the inside. Instead I sat there and felt empty – an emptiness like nothing I had ever felt before. It was a physical emptiness because he wasn't in my tummy anymore, and I wasn't holding him in my arms either, but it was an indescribably painful, emotional emptiness too. Just like that, my old friend numbness was back.

As I watched toddlers play in the surf and mothers sitting around us on the beach holding their babies and rocking them in their prams, I wanted to scream out, *I'm a mother too, you know!* I wanted to tell them that I had given birth to my beautiful baby boy only last week, and yet here I was, without him. I realised that people were looking at my husband and I as a young couple, holding hands on the beach, and were probably thinking we were having a lovely, relaxing break, just us two. Perhaps they thought we were on a fun mini-break or a honeymoon? They had no idea of the reality we were living in; the pain, the sorrow and the pure misery that we both felt in that moment. I felt anger towards the world that people viewed us as 'just a couple'; I was a mother, we were parents. Yet because our son had been taken away from us so soon, so unfairly, to the rest of the world it was as though he never existed. I hated this feeling; it made my grief for Teddy intensify.

I didn't want him to be erased from history and I knew that surely there must be other mothers out there like me, other mothers going through this.

Back at the holiday cottage, I began my search. My search that I hoped would make me feel less alone. I can remember Googling 'My baby has died' and such like, just to see what would come up. Strangely that very weekend I came across a blog that had been shared on Facebook. It was one of those strange degrees of separation moments. The blog had been written by a friend of my best friend's good friend (follow me?) and her daughter had been stillborn just seven months previously. I was just over a week into Teddy's loss and she was months ahead of me, and I read her words and felt like she was talking directly to me. In that moment, all of my emotions were normalised. Most importantly I didn't feel alone anymore. She had only just started her blog and (I suppose like myself many months later) she had been waiting for a time when she felt strong enough to share her story, and was ready to try and help others.

I wanted to find her, give her a hug and tell her that all of her words had resonated with me so deeply. It was as if, all in that moment of reading her words, I realised I wasn't alone. That someone before me had already experienced all of these new emotions I was wading through, and that I wouldn't be the last to feel them either. She was writing things that I was certain only a bereaved mother could write; only a bereaved mother could truly understand the enormity of those emotions. She gave me an enormous amount of hope, that there was a way forward from this.

When I told Nico what I had found and how much it was helping me to read it, he looked so relieved. He had seen me start to spiral into a very dark place, a lonely place where I knew none of my friends, not even the closest ones, could even begin to understand. You can't understand it unless you have been through it, unless you have felt those things yourself. So that was it, that was the answer for me; I needed to find more of us, other women who were going through this pain and who could understand how I was feeling.

Nico and I decided to head home early. The cottage was ours for a few more days, but we couldn't face it; both of us agreed the best thing to do would be at home. I wanted to feel differently, to feel as though the break away from it all had helped. It was too soon though, and no amount of magic wand waving was going to help the way that either of us felt.

Chapter 7

A New Normal

THE DAY THAT WE LEFT FOR CORNWALL I HAD DECIDED TO START A JUST GIVING DONATIONS PAGE FOR THE NICU – I WAS SPURRED ON BY THE BEREAVEMENT MIDWIFE'S DISBELIEF AT MY IDEA. In my depths of purposelessness, I felt the sudden urge to do something positive, to feel as though I was announcing to the world what had happened to Teddy, but also trying to help the hospital and staff that had tried so desperately to save him. I shared it on my Facebook and my Instagram. I don't really know what I expected, but I certainly didn't expect what happened next.

I watched as the total of donations began to rise. I had simply and candidly explained on the page what had happened to us that previous week – about Teddy's entrance and all-too-soon exit from this world. I had written about all the hospital had done for us and how they had tried to help Teddy. Our friends, family and acquaintances began to read our story and the donations came in thick and fast. By the time we arrived in Cornwall, we had raised over £7,000 in a matter of hours. The following day it was £10k and it continued to rise. I suddenly felt as though we were doing something; something positive in Teddy's name. Of course it didn't make me happy, I was too in the depths of grief to feel any flicker of happiness, but I felt something, a positive change in events that stuck with me.

I had been watching the total of our fundraising going up over the course of our stay and we had got to almost £14,000 in donations. I couldn't believe that so many people cared, that so many people wanted to help the neonatal unit for what they had done for Teddy. It was the one thing that kept me going in my darker moments; looking at the total and feeling like there was going to be hope for other babies. I kept saying to Nico that if we could save just one couple from this feeling, then we would have done a good job.

★

We arrived home to a house full of dead flowers, and it suited my mood. Cornwall hadn't been a break, but it had been a bubble. The cards had mounted up further, letters from the hospital and various charities wanting to help us had arrived. We had landed right back into the baby loss world, immersed in its sadness and isolation. After a few hours of sorting and unpacking I felt deflated and found myself sobbing uncontrollably again.

Nico had to go back to work at the end of that week as he had already been off work for his two-week paternity leave. We were heading into our third week and I wasn't ready to be left alone. I still hadn't seen any of our friends or neighbours – how could I be left on my own all day to deal with this, and how was he expected to work? The anxiety was so strong, it made me feel a wave of sickness.

That night, convinced that I too was going to die, now I knew the unthinkable was possible, I was too scared to close my eyes and go to sleep. Teddy should have been two weeks old, but he wasn't here. Nico had had to hold me and reassure me, stroke my head and tell me it was going to be OK, until I eventually passed out from the exhaustion and emotion. I also had a pain in my leg after the journey back from Cornwall.

When I called the midwives office they insisted that I came back in to be checked over by a doctor, just in case the leg pain was anything more sinister than it should be. They thought I might have a blood clot, deep vein thrombosis, which I now know isn't that uncommon either – honestly, as women it's a wonder that any of us actually sign up for this!

After a few hours back in the bereavement room of the maternity wing, and after tests and scans, it was confirmed that I didn't have anything wrong with me. It appeared that the throes of grief and shock had convinced my mind that there was something wrong with me too, and there wasn't, other than grief. I kept apologising to the midwives and the doctors, I felt so foolish and embarrassed that I had wasted their time. They all just kept reassuring me and saying that they would rather be safe than sorry. It didn't help though, I felt like they were just saying that to save me feeling like the neurotic person I had become in the two weeks since Teddy was born. Was this just me now?

This proved to me that I wasn't ready for Nico to go back to work in two days' time. I don't think he was either, but at the same time I think he needed to busy his mind, to get back to 'normal'. He wasn't recovering from the physical element of a nine-month pregnancy like I was, he wanted to focus himself away from the grief and he assured me that he wanted to go back to work. The sooner he faced those people in the office, then the sooner the painful part of telling them what had happened would be over. A kind colleague had sent a round robin email to all of the relevant people in his office, and many of them had also taken the time to make a donation to our fundraising page. For a huge corporation they did incredibly well, as did my place of work – sending flowers and cards, and letters from HR offering their support in any way possible. We both felt incredibly lucky that we were being so well looked out for in every aspect of our lives.

The day before Nico returned to work, we tried to take Boris out on a walk in the park that afternoon. I say tried mainly because it ended in me being frozen to the spot on the path next to the river and proclaiming to Nico that, 'I can't move.' I think this was my first real experience of an anxiety-led panic attack; well, my first in public. I soon realised that the bedtime terror and the feelings that surrounded my fear of going to sleep were also rooted from this anxiety. This moment though, in the park, compounded for me that this whole 'getting back to normal' journey wasn't going to be a case of me just getting out there and facing the world, like Nico was trying to do. What if I couldn't? I didn't feel comfortable being in a park where I might pass people; people with children, expectant mothers, other dog walkers that might want to chat. All of them terrified me.

Nico managed to lead me out of the park and to a much quieter place we sometimes walked, near to the canal through some fields. I stood in the fields and sobbed (this was becoming a habit) as I held on to him. I kept saying, 'What's wrong with me?' I was truly terrified that I would never feel able to face the world. Everything felt louder, harsher, brighter and I couldn't cope. I have since read a lot about grief and the feelings that surround it, and have learned that all of these reactions are perfectly normal and justifiable. The world can be a very loud and brash place, but we tend to tune out of that when we are busy leading our lives. When loss happens, we stop – it quite literally stops us in our tracks – and we find ourselves unwillingly tuning back in to all of those noises and goings on around us. I found the outside world deafening, and I didn't feel safe.

I knew I needed to make adjustments to my days to cope. If Nico was going back to work then I would need to make I made sure I did 'small' things like walking

Boris. The day he returned to work my parents came to look after me. I began to think that I would spend eternity being babysat by various family members until I was ready to face the world again. The second day I had arranged for one of my closest friends to come and visit me. She was the only person I felt I could face. I knew she wouldn't be too weird with me and that she would be the kind of person who could just take it in her stride – I needed some normality.

She came with food and trashy magazines – both a welcome escape! She asked about Teddy, asked how I was physically and she wanted to talk about his birth and all of the happy parts of what had happened. We talked about the sad parts too, and I remember telling her not to be afraid to ask questions, that no question was too silly, and that I wouldn't get angry or upset with her for asking. It enabled me to talk openly about Teddy right from the start, and this was a tactic I went on to use when I first saw any of my friends after Teddy's death.

No one knew what to say, of course they didn't; and I don't think there is a right thing to say when someone loses a child or loved one. I knew from the cards, texts, letters and messages on social media that everyone was there, ready to see us and be there for us.

Some of our friends had done the most thoughtful of things, dropping a survival hamper to our doorstep. It had home-cooked food, essentials and beautiful letters of support. They had simply dropped it to the door and then sent a text to let us know it was there; there was no expectation to see us, or for us to have to feel pressured into seeing people when we weren't ready.

I knew when we were ready, that everyone would be there. I just couldn't face much; not just yet. It still didn't feel real to me, and the longer I kept myself to myself, the longer I felt I could hold on to that little piece of the 'old me' that everyone knew. Not this new existence. *Nobody needs to see her*, I thought.

Chapter 8

When the Dust Begins to Settle

AS THE DAYS WENT ON, I REALISED THERE HAD TO COME A MOMENT WHEN THE REAL WORLD WAS LET BACK INTO OUR LIVES. Nico had returned to work just three weeks after Teddy had been born, meaning it hadn't been three weeks since our son had passed away and normal working life had resumed. I know that if he had asked he would, of course, have been granted more time off to give him extra time to heal. Strangely, I felt that was the last thing he wanted. He wanted to be back in the thick of work, as a form of escapism from what had just happened. When a baby dies everyone rallies around the mother and in many ways I understand that, as I was the one whose hormones were telling her each day that there was a baby missing from her arms, that something had gone monumentally wrong. My concerns were all for my husband though, and how he was coping. We were in constant communication throughout the days when he was at work, and his bosses were really understanding in allowing him to work from home if he needed.

Family members and friends were working the rota of looking after me. I had felt strong enough to see a few of my best friends, but I was still communicating with most of the outside world by text message. I would see my phone flashing with incoming calls and often ignore them – I knew that those calls came from a place of love and concern, but I couldn't face them. How would those conversations go? Like every other I had faced: 'How are you feeling?' Basically, fucking terrible. So bad in fact that I can't really articulate it and I can't say anything that I think will make you understand it. Too harsh? It just felt exhausting; a constant cycle of being asked how I was feeling, when I would have thought the answer was pretty obvious. I knew people were trying to help, I knew that, but I found myself regurgitating the same lines as answers, like tedious news soundbites where I was trying to top-line the overwhelming feelings of grief when your child dies. It was like ripping off a plaster again and again, each time wincing in pain as the reality set in that Teddy was gone. Other people just wanted to hear our voices, to see that we were still physically standing; that we were 'OK'. They only had to have that conversation once though; I was repeating it again, and again, and *again*. I felt like a broken record, trying to reassure everyone that we were OK and that I trusted the doctors would find out what had happened to Teddy.

That was the other problem – we still didn't actually know. We had no idea what made Teddy so poorly, or why he had stopped breathing the first night after he was born. They had ruled things out though; it wasn't sepsis, or group B strep. He hadn't inhaled any meconium during his birth, his placenta all looked normal. I kept drawing my mind back to what his consultant had said about his metabolic system – that was my one glimmer of hope, that she was on to something, and I really trusted that she was.

Teddy had gone to the coroner after he died, before he was released to the funeral directors in our local town. Instead of spending those early weeks after his birth liaising with health visitors and taking him for check-ups, I was on the phone to the coroner's office every other day waiting for an update of when he would be released. They were so sensitive, and kind and helpful. We knew we had weeks to wait for the cause of death, possibly even months, so being able to have the funeral before then was definitely the right thing for us. I wanted Teddy to be at peace. He had spent almost every hour of his little life being monitored, poked and prodded; this was his time to rest.

Once we got the go-ahead to organise the funeral we went to a funeral director's in the high street, just a short walk from our house. It was the weirdest experience. I have to say I had never even really noticed there was a funeral director there – why would I? No enticing window display or reason for me to just pop in as I passed by on my way through town.

As we walked in we were greeted by an older lady with a kind face. She asked us if she could help and we explained we needed to organise a funeral and would like their assistance. She led us through to a grey-looking office with hefty mahogany furniture filling ever available wall space. We were sat at an equally hefty mahogany desk, and she settled herself in the chair opposite.

'I'll need to start with a few questions, if that's OK with you? Now, who is the deceased that you are organising the funeral for?'

Both of us were stunned into silence. I looked down as those hot, heavy tears returned to make streams down my face. Nico, after a long pause, said, 'Our son, Teddy.' Quickly followed by, 'He was a baby.'

I don't think people who work arranging funerals are easily shocked or saddened; I mean, I imagine you become pretty accustomed to mortality, but her face said it all. 'I am so sorry.' She seemed to almost whisper it as she hastily pushed the box of tissues that had been to the side of the desk in my direction, and she reached out her hand to squeeze mine. She then said, 'Are you sure you are both OK to do this now? I can give you some more time; or you can just fill these forms in and bring them back?'

She couldn't have been lovelier to us. It made me cry even more. She explained all of the ins and outs of how it would work. They would arrange the crematorium, the car and look after Teddy until the day of the funeral. We were, of course, free to visit him as we wished, but we had long since decided that wasn't what we wanted. All we needed to do was contact the vicar, and drop an outfit to them that we wanted Teddy to wear. We were free to arrange our own flowers if we wished. After we gave all of the information we had, we left some 30 minutes later and were both an utter mess. No parent should *ever* have to do that.

We were put in touch with the local vicar, who arranged to come to the house that weekend and see us. Teddy's funeral was to be held a month after he had been born. It felt like a lifetime of waiting in limbo, so these little steps to making plans for him became vital parts of our early healing. We knew we didn't want a big funeral, we wanted our closest family only – something we agreed on with no discussion needed. In some ways I felt so guilty that we were almost pushing our friends away during a time that they only wanted to help us, but we had to do what felt right for us, and for Teddy, and we both agreed that this was it.

When the vicar came to the house he was also warm and friendly. He told us he was a dad, and a grandad, and I felt like he spoke to us as both of those, and not from a position within the Church. It definitely made us both warm to him more as neither of us are hugely religious. (I mean, I believe there is something, a power or energy that surrounds us all and helps us to carry on when we think we cannot, but I wasn't really set on the big man in the sky and the set of pearly gates idea.) My husband and I were married in a church, mainly because we lived in fear of offending grandparents if we didn't, and we much preferred the church vows of marriage. We make it to church for all the usual occasions: births, deaths, marriages and Christmas. I never prayed when Teddy was poorly – I know that other people did on our behalf, but I think I asked the universe to make it better. What I am saying is that, and I am not even entirely sure why I am telling you this, I wouldn't call myself a fully paid-up member of Christianity. The vicar didn't seem to care about that though.

I was honest with him – I told him I didn't think Teddy was an angel, but I did hope that his energy continued to live on. To which he replied, 'Of course it does. He lives in both of you. Remember that this grief won't last forever, but love does.'

To this day, whenever anyone asks me where Teddy is, I tell them that; I think it is the most meaningful thing that anyone has ever said to me, just when I needed it.

⭐

The days that led up to the funeral were nothing less than torturous. I felt as though the occasion was a means to some kind of end, although I didn't see how this living nightmare would be at an end just because we had had a funeral. Each day felt so long. Nico took the day before off work – we were both a mess. In the weeks that that had passed since Teddy had died I had written many letters to him, of how I felt and how I missed him. By getting all of those thoughts and emotions down onto a page it felt as though I was talking to him. That day I remember feeling an overwhelming need to write, and I wrote him a letter about how I was dreading the next day.

That feeling, that build-up, has come to be a familiar one in our lives since. Every 'first' and every 'milestone' we have come to since has been preceded with that pang of dread, that overwhelming sense that something awful is about to happen. The difference these days is that I can see it coming and I am aware of the impact it will have on my life while it is there; in those early days, it was crippling.

The morning of the funeral was like most others since Teddy had died. I got up, showered and had my breakfast; tried to choose what to wear. I can tell you that trying to pick the 'right' outfit for my baby's funeral is probably a fashion low point for me. Black says 'grieving mother' and colourful, although hopeful, seemed too bright – *too* optimistic. I know that fashion should be the last thing on anyone's mind in this situation, but sadly, for me, like most occasions in my life (and as a trait I have inherited from my mother) I seem to recall the details of almost all occasions based on what I was wearing! I mean *who* does that? I could see how bloody ridiculous the whole thing was as I stood in front of the mirror, trying to shoehorn my newly softened (squidgy) post-partum body into anything that would actually fit and not make me feel even worse, if that was at all possible. I decided on the palest of blush pinks pleated chiffon midi-skirt (actually a maternity one I had bought for a friend's daughter's christening two months previously) and I wore an ivory short-sleeved silky top with big, brightly coloured blooms all over it. It's fair to say that I went with the whole 'hope and optimism' vibe. At least I was trying.

My parents, brothers and sisters-in-law arrived at the house that morning, and we all drank coffee, talked and laughed. That is something I will always love my family and be so very grateful for; we seem to have the ability to crack jokes and laugh even in the darkest of times. Even more so if anything. It's like this incredible human spirit that we are all bound by, and are able to still laugh and see light, even through the heavy tears.

I think we have my parents to thank for that, and I can most certainly thank my two older brothers for my resilience and good humour when other people take the piss.

We walked the ten-minute walk to the church, where we met Nico's parents and his sister and her husband. My sister-in-law gave me the tightest of hugs as we walked down the cobbled lane outside the church, and told me we'd get through it. The funeral director's car was outside, but I couldn't see Teddy's coffin. It wasn't a hearse, it was just a normal black car – I know now because Teddy was in such a little box, he didn't need a hearse. The kind vicar was waiting for us at the door, and hugged us both tightly before we followed him to the front of the church. I remember him saying, 'There is no rush, we can absolutely start when you are ready, and not before.'

Like with most things in recent weeks, I wanted to get going, to make sure it was over. I have no idea why, but it was almost as if I thought the pain might lessen once this was done. Nico squeezed my hand and the music started. Teddy was carried in, in his tiny white box, by one man; he cradled it in his arms in front of him with such care. The words of Ellie Goulding singing 'How Long Will I Love You' echoed around me, and Teddy was placed so carefully in front of us all. On top of his coffin lay one beautiful wreath from us all made up of cornflower blue hydrangeas, white gypsophila and eucalyptus – my favourites. We had it made by the same florist who had created our wedding flowers two years previously. I don't think she quite believed it when I got in touch and asked her to create something for Teddy, explaining in an email what had happened. I wanted to try and create as many connections as I could between him and us, and this was one of them. It made me so happy that she was able to help, and the wreath, from his family, looked utterly perfect.

The vicar spoke, again with such warmth, and I could see he felt true sadness too as he looked down at the little white box that lay in front of him. He spoke about family and togetherness, and he spoke once more as a father and grandfather, one who was reaching out to a family who were beyond broken and trying to help them. Everyone sobbed. I can remember looking around at everyone's faces as he spoke, trying to take it all in and remember what this looked like, what it *felt* like. It was the very last time I was going to be physically in the same room as Teddy; the time before had been when we had been with him as he took his last breaths. This was it, the very last time he would be here. As in his last moments, I found myself trying to photographically remember what this looked like, where everyone was seated. It sounds so crazy now, but I suppose it was the little control that I had in the midst of the most out of control situation I have ever been in.

Teddy's Aunty Zoe, Nico's sister, spoke so beautifully as she read a piece she had written for Teddy. She spoke so fondly of love for her brother and of what family meant, and how she would think of Teddy as part of our lives forever more. It was abundantly clear to me that this church was bursting with so much love for our little boy; that he would be so missed and so loved, forever. The vicar repeated that line, 'Grief doesn't last forever, but love does.' I could feel that already.

They carried Teddy out to more music chosen by us, and from that moment on I don't remember much of anything. As I stood, my legs were physically shaking and tears blinded me. Nico squeezed both my hands and I tried to watch for every last second to see the coffin as they carried it away. I wanted to see him until I couldn't anymore. My mother-in-law followed the vicar out of the church, a single rose in her hand from their garden that she wanted to go with Teddy to the crematorium. With that, I broke down. Nico held me, and I hung on to him for dear life as we both sobbed.

After some time, we all left the church and walked next to the river to a quiet place we had booked for lunch. As we walked out of the church Nico said to me, 'Nothing will ever feel as bad as today did. We have come through it. It has to get better.'

Oh, how I hoped he was right.

Chapter 9

Benchmark of Shit

MY RESOUNDING MEMORIES OF THAT DAY ARE ONES OF LOVE, SUPPORT AND LAUGHTER; NOT THE SADNESS. I think I was learning (still am) to focus on the things we did have. For us that was incredible family and friends – we were surrounded by so much love, that was clear. Nico took the rest of the week off work. It was like we were both recovering from a hangover of sadness, both feeling weary and weighed down by it all.

I don't think it was until after that week that I really started to think about how we would even contemplate moving forward from losing Teddy. The limbo was coming to an end, we were coming into July and, as much as I didn't want it to, the summer was happening. It was that following week we found out that Nico was to travel to New York for work that month. It hit me that he wasn't going to be here – that I would be alone, without him next to me at night for the first time since Teddy had died. We had known that his NY trips that year were going to be inevitable, but I had envisaged myself with a new baby, and being able to get my mum to stay with us and look after both me and the baby while Nico was away. The reality was quite different, and I chose to retreat back to my parents to escape the emptiness of our house.

*

Thankfully, in the UK, a mother is still on maternity leave after the death of a baby. You are legally entitled to the maternity leave that was agreed with your employer on your departure from work – this is definitely something we don't talk about enough. For me, I was staring down the barrel of another ten months off work. Of course, I could go back sooner if I wanted to, and many well-meaning friends asked if that was my plan. The thought of going back, facing everyone – especially in a sales job where I had to face different people and re-tell the whole sorry story each day – quite frankly made me feel physically sick. I was safer at home; happier spending some time recovering mentally, physically and emotionally from a full-term pregnancy and the trauma of losing our son.

I was very fortunate that my work contract meant that I benefitted from a generous package – this meant that at least we didn't have anxiety about money on top of everything else. That really was one of the small things that helped so much, and I just wish it was the case for everyone who has a child, let alone loses that child. I felt very lucky that I was able to take that time that I needed, as much as other people may have thought it would 'do me good' to get back to it. Personally, I couldn't think of any good that would come from forcing myself unnecessarily into a situation that would worsen my recovery. I was staying put, and I didn't feel *any* guilt about that.

It was in our home, my sanctuary, that I hid out as the weeks passed after Teddy's death. It had become, even more so than ever, my safe place. I suppose we all have our passions, the hobbies that we might like to pursue more but work and general life takes over. For me that had always been our home. My nesting instinct had gone wild in the lead up to Teddy being born, but now he was gone the results felt wasted. His nursery was still there, perfect and untouched;

a beacon of hope in our time of darkness. The rest of the house? Well, much of it had been 'done' too, but my empty arms and broken heart gave me a reason to get stuck in. It helped busy my mind and keep my hands, which should have been caring for a new baby, busy too. In between spending days with friends and my mum it was the welcome distraction that I needed. I painted furniture and framed prints that had been lying around (very much on my to-do list for months). I began redecorating rooms and collecting new pieces for each one that I could upcycle – I did things I could give my care and attention, that I could lovingly restore to try to find some kind of missing fulfilment in my life.

As the summer progressed, so did other people's lives. My phone rang far less, and the text messages became less frequent. There were a few people's reactions that hurt me and shocked me, mainly those ones who failed to say anything at all, even though they had been so keen to send me messages when I had been expecting Teddy. I was dumbfounded that people could fail to say anything, not reach out with one word.

The more I grew to understand how the world views

the loss of a baby, the more I understood why that was their reaction. Was I sad? Yes, but I wasn't angry at them. Some people simply do not know what to say, so they leave it; in the hope that an easier time will come, a window of opportunity to get in touch or say the right thing. Then that time frame gets longer, and that window of opportunity gets smaller, and before they know it months have passed and they haven't even acknowledged that your child has died.

I think the subject makes them feel awkward, but I would remind them that the awkwardness they feel in that one fleeting moment of talking to you about it, is nothing compared to that awkwardness you carry for the rest of your life as a bereaved parent. My one piece of advice to those people is pick up the phone, send a text – send a bloody pigeon if you have to. Just a 'I'm so sorry to hear. I am here for you.' That's all. Failing that, just throw some emoji hearts their way in a message; even that is better than silence.

There were a few people that said nothing to me at all, and then casually text me about something months later and still failed to say the words, 'I am sorry to hear that your son died.' Them ignoring it, acting like Teddy hadn't existed, hurt even more – it wasn't what I needed or wanted, but they didn't know I felt like that, because they had never bothered to communicate with me.

There will always be those friends who are always there, though – the ones who called even when I'd had enough, who mentioned Teddy whenever they could and tried their hardest to keep us going. When most people went back to their normal lives after the initial shock of hearing he had died, it's safe to say that our true friends were still there. They understood we were still struggling. They knew that socialising was off the cards for the foreseeable, but that we would come to quiet lunches at people's houses when we could, only because we couldn't just stay locked up in the house forever being miserable bastards together. They didn't get offended when we weren't immediately up for nights out or weekends away, or when we couldn't face a wedding or a christening in the first year after Teddy died. They got it. I will be *forever* thankful for that.

They were also the friends who understood that a pregnancy announcement from them might not be met by raucous congratulations from our corner. Not because we weren't happy for them, but because it was just too much, too soon, and we were just a little bit broken still. No one wants to be that friend who can't be genuinely happy for someone when they share the happiest news, but losing a child brings a whole new layer of complex emotions into your life, ones that I won't ever truly understand. Of course, I wished them a healthy, happy pregnancy and most importantly a baby to come home with at the end of it; but mine didn't, and sometimes everything seemed like a constant reminder of that.

It won't come as a surprise to anyone when I say that friends are such an important part of your healing and recovery when you go through something shocking in life. I suppose the problem I encountered was that my friends, as much as they wanted to understand how I felt having lost Teddy, couldn't – quite simply because they had never experienced it themselves. Some of them sobbed so hard I could see the pain in their faces as they tried to imagine what it might feel like. Human nature never quite allows us to imagine fully the emotions of the unthinkable, does it?

I knew that my friends wanted to help me *so much*. It wasn't their fault that I felt a lurch in my stomach every time I saw one of them holding their baby or pushing their child in a pram; they weren't to be blamed in any way. I began to feel like the worst person on the planet. I was so angry at the universe for taking

Teddy away from us, for allowing this to happen to our family. Every new pregnancy announcement from friends or family felt like the final twist of the knife. I wanted, so badly, to be as happy for everyone as the old me would have been for such wonderful news, but I was just broken by Teddy's loss and I didn't know how to fix it.

★

During the months after Teddy died, it became blindingly apparent that we were now the benchmark for other people's version of 'when shit happens'. I have to say this isn't a fabulous place in which to exist. It somehow made things sting a little more; a constant reminder of just how bad a turn our lives had taken.

What I mean by this, for example, is: friends would be talking and explaining something bad that has happened to them or perhaps a friend, and then they would quickly interject with an emphasised, 'Of course *it's nothing* compared to what you've been through.'

There we have it – losing a child instantaneously makes you the benchmark of shit. Wonderful.

I think people feel guilty; they feel bad for saying something is bad or unfair when they see what we've been through. I don't want people to ever feel guilty for that. Shit happens, that is life; trust me, I have waded through it for over two years of my life now. I guess that I just began to accept their words. Like with so many other things, they didn't realise that they were serving you with a constant reminder of just how awful things were in your life. If anything, I suppose I should be thankful that I have friends who are thoughtful and emotionally intelligent enough to realise just how life-changing losing a child must feel. They could see the devastating impact that losing Teddy had caused in every single aspect of our lives, and they appreciated that. They weren't about to belittle its enormity by comparing it to something else, and we appreciated that.

✦

One of my resounding observations was the difference in peoples' reaction to Teddy's death – that difference in understanding and of knowing what to say and what not to, and when. There most certainly isn't a textbook from which any of us can take instruction, and believe me when I say that sometimes I wish there had been. I found some people's desire to relate and to tell me that they somehow 'understood' how it felt to lose a child, when quite clearly they did not, was utterly bizarre. Some of the kindest messages and emails that I received were the ones that quite simply stated 'I can't even begin to imagine. . .' That's correct, you *can't*. Just like I can't begin to imagine what it feels like to lose a parent or a sibling. I wouldn't even pretend to know what that feels like by saying to a friend who has lost a parent, 'I kind of know what it feels like because. . .', I have no idea, absolutely *none*.

I think the problem with child loss, other than the glaringly obvious problem that your baby has died, is that it is so utterly shocking to people that they don't quite know what to say. It's when something that should be the happiest event on earth, the arrival of a new life, a new family member, turns into the worst event, the saddest – the unimaginable. I think that flips our brain into panic mode and many people think that they need to try to understand as opposed to just sympathise with the situation.

I tried my absolute hardest to focus on that and to remember it each time I spoke to someone new, or for the first time after losing Teddy. I accepted that they didn't mean it, and I knew that, of course, they couldn't ever truly understand how it had felt for us to lose our firstborn son. That sometimes they might just fill the air with words, so as not to let the silence become too deafening; and that something, anything, is better than nothing.

Then, for some reason unbeknown to me, there were the people who seemed to be clamouring to be my 'friend'. Yep, that's right, at a time in my life when I couldn't have felt less enthusiastic about seeing my actual friends, let alone finding new ones, there they all were. The people I had gone to high school with some 15 years ago, the ones I had worked with for a brief period many moons ago, the ones who were a friend-of-a-friend (who had never actually met me, but had heard what happened and, you know, obviously needed to be there for me). I didn't *know* any of these people, many of them I doubted whether I would even utter a 'Hi' to if I were to bump into them in a supermarket, yet here they were, asking me if I ever wanted to go for a coffee and a 'catch-up'?

What? Now? When my son has just died? No thanks, I would literally rather do anything else in the world right now. Did they not understand the enormity of what had just happened? Of course I wouldn't just be popping for a casual coffee and a chat with a virtual stranger when it was all I could do most mornings to actually swing my legs around to the side of the bed and actually face my reality. I had no idea what these people were thinking or why they ever thought it was a good idea to do that, out of the blue, just because my son had died.

The more time has passed, I think I know the answer now: people were shocked, so shocked that it stopped them in their tracks. It made them think how fortunate they were, how lucky that it hadn't happened to them or someone in their family. That's what we do, isn't it? We hear about something bad that has happened and we think, *Gosh, I can't even imagine what that must be like.* Our minds won't let us go there, but we are glad it wasn't us.

Those people, the ones I didn't really know, they wanted to see me – to talk to me and know that I was OK, still living and breathing – as that way, in their minds, the shock and sadness wouldn't be so bad for *them*. They would be able to move on with their lives without so much as a pang of guilt that it hadn't happened to them. What about *me* though? I still had to live with it, had to carry on and live each day in this unexpected narrative of motherhood. Would I be going to 'hang' with them, so they could feel a little bit easier about that? No thanks, I'll give that a miss.

There are also the 'grief thieves', as I have coined them. The ones who love to make it all about *them*.

We all encounter them in life – someone dies and it becomes all about how much they knew them and how sad they are about it all. The truth is, other than our immediate family, no one had met Teddy; no one *knew* him. This meant that there was nothing tangible to hold on to as memories for people, so I was that 'thing'. They needed to see me, to tell me how sorry and/or shocked/saddened they were at our loss. They needed to feel like they had acknowledged to me how bad it was for them.

The truth was, I only cared how his death had affected us and our family, no one else. Yes, it was lovely that people reached out, sent cards and flowers, but I couldn't really have given a toss about how much it had affected them. The truth of the matter was that they could go about their normal day tomorrow. They could go to work, or pop to the shops or do whatever the hell else it was that was on the agenda the next day. I couldn't; not without that constant ache in my chest, not without feeling like I had an anvil hanging over my head that was about to drop, or without fearing I would burst into unstoppable, powerful tears at any given moment. Trust me when I say that this was the one time in my life when I really, *really* wished it hadn't been all about me, but sadly it was.

★

There were a couple of people who I chose to give time to outside of our family or immediate circle of friends, in the first six weeks or so after Teddy died. One was a fellow expectant mother, whose baby had also been born in May. We had exchanged numbers in the final weeks of pregnancy and agreed we would make an effort to perhaps meet up once the babies had arrived. I had texted her the week after Teddy was born to explain what had happened. She was kind and said she would tell the other mums who I had met. She sent her love and condolences, and the following week sent a message to see if I wanted to meet up. I think she was doing her best to make me feel less alone, and that just because Teddy wasn't here it didn't mean we couldn't still be friends.

A few weeks later we went for that coffee, she asked me how I was doing, and I cried a lot, but tried my best not to be an utter rain cloud of emotion. I met her baby, who was sweet and beautiful, as any newborn would be. I felt a lurch of jealousy in the pit of my stomach, but I told it to shut up; I didn't want to be *that* person. We chatted about my experience over those four weeks, and hers – both very different stories of being a new mum.

Then she said, 'When are you going back to work then?'

Just like that, when I thought I was talking to someone who might get it, I realised I wasn't.

'I'm sorry? My. . .my son just died. I'm not going back to work anytime soon,' I replied.

She seemed surprised, and asked me what I would do if I wasn't at work and I didn't have a baby at home. Thanks for reminding me. My body was recovering from a full-term pregnancy, just like hers was. My hormones were still all over the fucking place, just like hers. My son had died, and her baby was lying in a pram next to her, gurgling away happily. Yet I was the one who was expected to go skipping back into work?

I turned it on its head. 'So when will you go back?'

I don't think she was expecting that, and then proceeded to launch into an explanation of how she didn't know if she would, but was under pressure as she was the major breadwinner between her and her boyfriend, etc. I zoned out. I came for a chat with someone I thought I had connected with, someone I thought had cared about me in the wake of my son dying, and we were sat here chatting about going back to bloody work?! After a bit more chit-chat we went our separate ways and, suffice to say, we never hung out again.

I did see her though, and she saw me, about six weeks later. I had been walking Boris through the park on a hot August day and wearing my sunglasses, as not only were they required for obvious reasons but they acted as a mighty fine disguise kit, and shielded my face from onlookers when I (still) unexpectedly burst into tears in public. Out of the corner of my eye I saw a group of ladies with prams and sunshades, all with small babies; blankets spread across the floor next to the bandstand. They were enjoying a mum and baby get-together on a beautiful August day, why not? There she was, standing in the middle and bouncing her baby as if to rock him off to sleep.

As I approached them, I prepared to say hello and face my worst nightmare of a group of new babies with happy mums. In that moment she saw me, I know she did, and she turned her back away so that she was facing the group. I picked up my pace, carried on past and thought, *Phew, she's done me a huge favour.* Then, I heard it.

When she thought I was out of earshot she said, 'That's Elle, who I was telling you about.' I could feel their eyes burning into the back of my head. She had seen me, and yet she had *ignored* me, on purpose? Maybe it was because she thought it would be too awkward for me? Maybe it was too hard for her to think of a way to explain to them all how we knew each other?

There it was; the single most isolating moment of my new torturous reality so far. I felt as though I had been well and truly, unceremoniously kicked out of the Mummy Club. *You can't sit with us, because your baby died.* I felt so alone in that moment, so low. I cried all the way home – those hot, weighted tears again, streaming down my face. Why did I even care? I didn't really know her, and I didn't know any of them at all. It wasn't about that; I didn't want their pity anyway. I just wanted my son, and I wanted the outside world to see me as his mother.

Chapter 10

Helping Myself

(When No One Else Could)

I THOUGHT ABOUT HOW I MIGHT FIND PEOPLE WHO UNDERSTOOD WHAT I WAS FEELING. When we had left the hospital, we were sent away with a bundle of 'we are sorry your baby died' type leaflets. Yep, a bundle of leaflets. Of course there were the letters that had arrived too (Harry Potter style, flying through the letterbox) in the early days after Teddy had died, asking us to come along to X, Y, Z charity support groups, but I had been so thick in the depths of grief that I hadn't even wanted to talk to anyone, let alone a room of bloody strangers, about how our son had died. I binned the letters and then regretted it when I was ready to talk. I wish someone had told me just to put them to one side, in case I changed my mind in the future.

Anyway, thanks to the handy leaflet bundle that I did keep, I knew that there were local Sands (Stillbirth and Neonatal Death) groups that we could attend if we wanted. I began to think about it, and whether we should go along to one. The concept felt so strange; and although I needed to talk to people who had also experienced the loss of their baby, I still couldn't get my head around forcing myself into a situation with a room full of people just because their baby had died too. I know they must be a huge support to so many, but I was totally freaked out. I spoke to Nico and he agreed; he said it was the last thing he wanted to do. Phew, I thought I was about to be the one holding us back on what we 'should' be doing. (For anyone who has recently lost and is worrying that they are not doing the right thing or speaking to the right people – just do what feels right. You do you. We all process things differently.)

All of this left me at a bit of a stumbling block. OK, so you want people who understand how you feel, but you're not prepared to actually go along to anything that will actually bring you face to face with other people who have lost their baby too? Yep, pretty much. Awkward bugger, aren't I? I racked my brains as I frantically Googled for answers – Google had never let me down before, it wasn't about to start now, surely? I found a link back to a Sands support group on Facebook. *Perfect*, I thought, access to a virtual world of people who understood me. You had to be approved to join, so I asked and waited. It was a private page and I was so keen to see what was there. I was hoping to see lots of positive, inspirational parents, sharing their stories and telling me it was going to be OK.

Finally. My group approval happened the next day, but it was less than a week before I left that group. I was looking for understanding, togetherness and positivity at a time of utter despair, but all I found were people saying how unfair life was and sharing photos again and again of their deceased children. I understood that it was perhaps the only place they felt safe to do so, and that those photos of their beautiful children were theirs to share with the world if they chose, but the feed was just that. Dead babies mixed with 'Why is life so shit?'. It wasn't the uplifting vibe I needed in my life, to say the least.

But perhaps my attitude was different to everyone else's. Oh god, perhaps I was totally alone in the way I was grieving Teddy. *No, that can't be right*, I thought. *Nico gets it.* When he came home from work one evening that week, I told him that the group was utterly depressing and I would never find another mother who had lost a child and actually got how I was feeling. Other than just one blog I had found that belonged to a friend of a friend whose daughter had been stillborn the previous year, no one was writing anything that spoke to me in a positive way. Also, the blogger was expecting again, and I felt like I couldn't reach out to her – she had enough going on without me adding to her life with my own goings-on. I needed to find people who, like me, didn't have other children here, and whose baby, their firstborn, had been taken too soon, too. They just didn't seem to be out there. Not on the internet, anyway…

★

As the weeks went on I knew that I needed to help myself if I was going to feel better, whatever 'better' would become for me. To start with, it was as much a physical recovery as it was mental. My body felt battered from a full-term pregnancy. I had gained four stone while growing that tiny human and was still carrying a great deal of that. I felt heavy and slow, and that was definitely making my days that were laden with grief feel much heavier and much slower. After starting to leave the house again and walk Boris on my own each day, I quickly recognised a connection between how much I did each day, and then how much better I slept and felt the next day.

Now, when I say things 'I did', I don't mean physically or mentally taxing things; we are talking very small steps here. I mean going out for a walk or taking myself to the shops. As long as I navigated it in a way that meant it wasn't too busy, or noisy, I felt better for doing it. I knew that this feeling rippled out from the other things I made time for, too; a soak in the bath, painting my nails, taking time to lie in the sun and read a book. Self-care became very much a part of my life in those early weeks and months. As someone who had spent 16 years in the beauty industry, it should have been second nature, but I found myself consciously making time to ensure I did something for myself each day, to make myself feel better. This didn't have to mean anything lavish or spending lots of money – it could be as simple as doing some yoga stretches in the living room before I ate my breakfast in the morning. And it was starting to make all of the difference.

Of course, I had a reason to get out of the house, to make myself 'do life', as I had Boris. Boris made me smile, he gave me purpose – a purpose that I was so desperately missing from my life. When I didn't want to leave the house, all I had to do was look at his little face, his expectant expression that we would be heading out for our daily walk, and that was enough to make me do it. Day by day I stepped out of that front door, faced the world, breathed in fresh air and became part of daily life again. That was all down to him. On the tough days he was there for me to cuddle. He let me (and still does) cry heavy tears onto him that rolled off his little head, as I clung to each and every thought of Teddy. Anyone who ever says to me that Boris is 'just a pet' will never understand what he has done for us, and I honestly will never be able to repay his kind little soul for saving us. I am thankful for him every day, and I can see why so many people who experience loss go on to get a dog; they truly are little lifesavers.

I knew that I had to help myself in as many ways as I had the power, for my mental as well as physical well-being. I sought solace in many things that I thought *might* just help me. I had begun attending yoga classes twice a week when I was pregnant with

Teddy, and it had helped me to sleep, eased my joint pains and essentially made me feel like less of a lethargic pregnant whale. After Teddy died I was lucky to find a true friend in my yoga teacher, Louise; she wanted to hear all about Teddy and offered many kind and positive words in those early days and weeks. Once I felt strong enough I returned to her regular yoga classes. These were filled with new faces – not the room full of expectant mothers as I had become accustomed to – and they gave me yet another place in which to disappear. The practice of yoga isn't just about the physical, you are able to set an intention at the beginning of each class, with yourself, of what you want to achieve. In those first few classes I set the intention of strengthening both my body and my emotions, to help myself recover. I began practising yoga more regularly at home too, and it helped me face the difficult days with a more positive attitude. It has strengthened my post-partum body beyond my expectations, and allowed me to believe in it again.

★

Our home was, and has continued to be, a huge healing help for me. It enabled me to have a creative outlet during those early days of grief, and I am unsure how

I would have managed without it. Even now, when I have a day when I feel that cloud of anxiety creeping towards me, I always stop and take time to do things in the house that make me feel happy and calm. Whether that is moving bits and pieces around or painting a piece of furniture, it never fails to make me feel better. I suppose it comes down to control in some respects, but for me it is also just a way of feeling like I am busying my hands and, in turn, calming my anxious mind.

I often wonder whether a time will come when I don't need it as an emotional crutch anymore, or if it is now so engrained into me that we are destined to always live in a show home?! It really has made me realise that we all use these techniques, whatever ours may be, to help us though the darker days. If you're reading and you know what that feels like to need something that calms your mind and helps you see the positive in each day again, I really do hope that you too have found your 'thing'. Always be open to trying new 'things' too – I discuss more that have helped me in chapter 17. I believe that there are always brighter days to be had for all of us, no matter what we have been through; sometimes we just have to find those little extra things that help us get there. Sometimes we just have to be brave enough to help ourselves.

Chapter 11

The Friends I Never Knew I Needed

OF COURSE, THE VERY NEXT DAY AFTER I DECLARED SOCIAL MEDIA COULDN'T BE OF HELP TO ME, THAT THEORY WAS PROVEN COMPLETELY AND UTTERLY WRONG. Say what you will about how it's set to ruin our children's future as we all slowly lose the art of conversation and disappear into an eternity of mindlessly scrolling through smart phones – in the situation I found myself in, it was pretty bloody amazing.

I was using my Instagram account and Pinterest boards as a way of finding inspiration for new changes in the house, and losing myself in a little world of squares that came with no judgement. It was a world away from the pain I was feeling in real life. I happily scrolled through my Instagram feed while sitting in the safety of our garden, feeling the summer sunshine on my skin, and actually beginning to feel more human again as my body recovered from the shock.

I had used my Instagram account a couple of times to post photos of Teddy, to share our fundraising page and as a way to tell the wider world what had happened. It was like an extension of my Facebook page, I suppose. The only people who really followed me were friends and family, but over the months a few fellow pug owners or home interiors enthusiasts had joined them. With just a couple of hundred people following me, it felt like a safe space to share those photos of Teddy and a little of the grief we were experiencing. It was always met with love and positivity – never the heaviness of the 'sad crying emoji reaction face' that Facebook threw my way. I was tired of people's pity; it wasn't what I wanted. I wanted some to say, 'Yeah, that's really shit, but you're going to be OK. Brighter days are coming.' My tireless search had led me nowhere – until today.

I was scrolling through that Insta-feed with my morning coffee as I prepared myself for another day of busying myself. I dipped into the 'Instagram suggested' page and one of the first posts I was met with made me hold my breath. It was a photo of the side of a wall that was covered in graffiti with the word LONDON. The caption started, 'Over the past couple of weeks I have been trying to re-enter the world. . .' What continued were the words of a bereaved mother, who was trying her best to carry on and give hope to others. Her daughter, Orla, had been stillborn in May. *Just like me*, I thought, *she's like ME!* It was my eureka moment in my new reality of motherhood.

As I read her words and how she too was planning new routes to places, avoiding places with prams and pregnant women and (of course) wearing sunglasses at all times to mask the tears, I just thought, *Thank god, I am not alone.*

My thumbs hovered over my phone keypad as I thought about what to say. I wanted to tell her I was here too, that I understood; that Teddy had been born in May too. I tentatively punched out and posted a comment: 'I'm currently living through this journey too. Thank you for sharing and for being so brilliantly honest about the emotions and struggles you are going through. There is hope for us, stay strong. Xx'

I held my breath and then sighed a huge sigh of utter relief. I had made my first attempt to connect with someone I thought might actually get me. I don't know how the Instagram algorithm had done it, but it bloody well had; it had found me someone I could relate to and, by the looks of it, she only lived an hour away.

She replied, 'I'm so sorry for the loss of your beautiful Teddy. I hope that you are doing OK and have lots of love and support around you. I am starting to see the light of hope too. Lots of love and strength back at you.'

Michelle, her name was Michelle, and she had just begun to follow me on Instagram. I started to scroll through the names of the other women who had commented, and I began to follow them all; scanning their Instagram pages and seeing they too had a baby who was no longer there. Where had these women been? I felt like I was scratching the surface of something so much bigger, something that ran so much deeper than I had ever realised. I began reading all of their stories and posts, their fundraising pages, and seeing their positivity leap out of those little squares filled me with so much joy. I *wasn't* alone.

In a few hours I received a new message from Michelle. She told me she had read Teddy's story on our fundraising page, that she was so sorry and she hoped I was doing OK. She explained that her and a few other 'loss mums' were starting a WhatsApp group for support; all had lost babies in recent months. She asked if I wanted to be added, but also said she understood if it wasn't really 'my thing' and that she wouldn't be offended if I didn't want to be included. Hell, I had no idea what my 'thing' even was anymore. I felt so lost, but these women were throwing me a bloody lifeline, something to keep me afloat. I had to take it. 'Yes, yes please.' And with that I gave her my mobile number.

It was like blind dating for the ultimate anti-NCT group, but it felt *so* good! Michelle told me the names of the other girls in the group and I made sure I was following them all on Instagram too. I wanted to put faces to names, to understand their stories and know their babies' names. I wanted them to be people, not just numbers in my phone. Later that evening I was added to a WhatsApp chat with a bunch of random numbers I did not know. It was entitled 'Warrior Women', and let's just say I knew from then that these ladies were going to save me in my darkest hour.

'Hi Elle, welcome' came a random number. I realised that was Jess – she had also contacted me via Instagram earlier that day, after Michelle had told her I wanted in on the chat. She and her wife, Natalie, had their firstborn son Leo in January that year; Leo had been stillborn. Jess had sent me the kindest message through Instagram saying that Michelle's message to her had prompted her to go straight to our fundraising page and read Teddy's story. She explained how she had always wished that Leo would have been the last baby to have ever been lost and that it broke her heart each time she learned of another. Her words made me sob – all she wanted to do was stop this from happening to other families. *Me too*, I thought. Jess and Nat had already raised so much in Leo's name, they looked unstoppable in their resolve and positivity.

The WhatsApp chat was Jess's idea and she introduced everyone in the group. I wasn't sure then if everyone had met already, or if, like me, they had just stumbled across each other via social media. I later found out that a few had met at different things, but not everyone had met everyone, and that Michelle and I hadn't met anyone – as Orla and Teddy had only died very recently, we weren't really in the place for going to anything!

Aimee lived in Devon, her daughter Phoebe had died during labour in January that year. Emma lived in North London, but was from Manchester (through and through, and she will actually kill me if I don't mention that). Her daughter, Florence, had died during labour, also in January of that year. Sam lived near Manchester, and her son, Guy, had been stillborn in November 2015. She was an intensive care nurse and was already back at work – I marvelled at how strong that seemed to me. All of these women, their strength, positivity and the way they wanted to honour their children – it blew me away. So that was us: Jess, Nat, Michelle, Aimee, Emma, Sam and Elle. The Warrior Women. I finally felt as though I had found my tribe.

The messages that ensued over the coming days came thick and fast; it was like speed dating, but with seven of you all trying to get to know each other at the same time. I found it fascinating. All of us had had such different experiences, but all with the same final outcome: our babies weren't here. We got to learn each other's stories; we talked about our pregnancies, our husbands, our jobs, families and lives. We covered everything, and there was so much humour in among it all. My fears had been laced with the idea that connecting with any other women who had lost a child would automatically mean we would be duty-bound to only talk about the sadness, the shock and grief; but here we all were talking about the normal stuff too.

I felt so relieved that there was a place I could finally talk. Somewhere that people understood me, and where there was zero judgement. Had a shit day? Tell the Warriors. Friend just said something wildly inappropriate that proves once again they have no idea what it feels like? Tell the Warriors. Each time I went into that chat and said 'This has just happened. . .' It proved to me that I wasn't losing my shit in the real world; that my feelings were justified and that I wasn't the only one who felt that way. We all had things we needed to share – how our families communicated with us, how our husbands were coping, if we were speaking to any counsellors and how that was going. It didn't feel forced and there was no judgement; these girls became my friends within a matter of weeks. I felt like I knew them, and yet we had never even met one another.

By the end of August, we decided that it would be a good idea to meet up, and we arranged an official 'date' at the end of October, in London. For me it was a huge date in my diary. I hadn't been into London since before Teddy had been born. Given that it had been a place I had lived and worked until we moved to Surrey, and continued to commute into every day until I left for maternity leave, it felt like another world. I knew I had to go, that I had to meet the Warriors and overcome my anxieties to get there. It was just another 'first' that I had to overcome. I put 28th October in my diary and looked forward to meeting them all, if only to give them a hug and say *thank you*.

I told a few of my friends about the Warrior Women after I had got to know them. It's fair to say it was met with mixed reviews; some thought it was a brilliant way to connect with other women who had experienced the same thing, and yet I got a sense from others that they disapproved in some way, that the friends that I had should have been enough for me.

I know that didn't come from a bad place, not at all; in fact, quite the opposite. We all feel protective over our friends, don't we? We would do anything to help them, comfort them and ensure they overcome their struggles, but what if we can't? What if what they are facing is just too far removed from our capabilities to understand? That's losing a child – that's where the understanding stops, no matter how good a friend you are. The way I saw it was that the Warriors were helping where my other friends weren't able. They weren't a replacement or me breaking away to a new life, they were a way for me to continue trying to get back to some kind of the old version of myself without totally losing my shit along the way. The bonus part was that, from what I knew of them all so far, I really bloody liked them all as friends, regardless of whether they had lost children or not.

I also felt like it meant I could spend time talking to my other friends about normal stuff again, without feeling like I was constantly bleating on about how my baby had died, killing the vibe every time we met up. I knew none of them saw it like that, but that was how I was starting to feel – like everyone else had exciting news, fun lives and lots of laughter, and I was just in a limbo of having lost my son and *still* not knowing why. My friends would always ask how I was doing, would always talk about Teddy openly, but having the Warriors to talk to about the heavy stuff just made the time without other friends a little easier, and left me a little less guilt-ridden about always being the sad clown who turned up and ruined the party.

✦

After the weeks of summer came to a close and autumn rolled around, I found myself in October. October already? I don't think a day had gone past where I hadn't spoken to the Warriors – they had become the daily tonic I needed as I adjusted to this new normal. One thing had remained the same since May, though: we still didn't know how Teddy had died, and for that reason we still hadn't registered his birth or death. My story was a little different from all of the other girls in the group for that reason. Teddy had lived outside of me, and then died – on the NHS's time, I might add, which is why they were hell bent on finding out a cause if they were able. Which meant we were still tangled up in the anguish of trying to get some answers as to what had happened to him.

At the beginning of October that call from the coroner finally came, unexpectedly. I remember the day as I had been sitting outside a local café with my friend and her daughter after a walk in the park with Boris. We had decided to grab some lunch and make the most of the dwindling summer sun while it lasted. As we were waiting for our food my phone rang. I knew who it was as soon as I saw the number, and although it felt wholly inappropriate to take the call then, I had to; I couldn't wait another second longer and needed this limbo to be over.

All of the samples they had taken from Teddy had shown nothing, not one thing; months of growing cultures in a lab and absolutely nothing. However, the samples the consultant had taken from him when he was alive – the urine samples I remember them withdrawing from his catheter with a tiny syringe –

those had given us an answer. Just as his consultant had suspected, on that first day she met Teddy when he was admitted into the NICU, he did indeed have a metabolic condition. His was very, very rare; so rare in fact that they had never seen a case of it in the UK, and only a handful worldwide.

Teddy had something called 3 methylglutaric aciduria (or 3MGA), and they had only narrowed it down to perhaps two of five types. It meant that everything was poisonous to him, even the air he was breathing as soon as he was born – his little body couldn't process it and couldn't get rid of any toxins on its own.

How did he survive the whole pregnancy? I thought. The consultant told us at a later date that the placenta had been doing all the hard work for Teddy, processing everything that he couldn't and keeping him alive. My body had been keeping him alive. I have to say I feel pretty bloody proud of myself (and that grotesque placenta) for doing such a great job. It meant I got to meet Teddy, to hold him and smell him and feel the warmth of his skin on mine. If it hadn't been for that placenta then, well, who knows? All I know is that I will never look at one the same way again, no matter how harrowing that image of mine still is.

The coroner said the consultants at the hospital

would go over everything else in more detail in a meeting. For now, all I cared about was that we could register our son as a person; a person who lived and who died. And a few days later, we went to do exactly that. We had made our appointment at the registry office and drove up the leafy driveway on a sunny October morning. The sun shone brightly that day and I remember thinking it was a sign from Teddy that he didn't want me to feel sad. Of course, that didn't help much, I was pretty much in floods of tears the moment we stepped through the doors.

The staff at the office were brilliant and so caring, given the circumstances. It must be so difficult for them to ask such direct and blunt questions in a situation where they have two grieving parents in front of them; in fact it must be difficult with anyone who is grieving a loved one. The lady registrar promised she would make it as quick and pain-free as she could, and she wasn't lying. We were in and out within half an hour, two certificates in hand: birth and death. As I had sat in that office I looked around and took in every detail, the signs on the walls, the detail of the desk and chairs, the way the sun beamed through the window and bounced off the adjacent white wall filling the room with light. It felt so cruel, so earth-shatteringly cruel, that we had to do this. I made a promise to myself that the next time we went there, to that room, it would be to register the birth of a 'take home baby', as I had come to call them.

The certificates were there in black and white. Edward Constantine Wright, our little Teddy, had been born on 16th May 2016 and left this world on 19th May 2016. We drove home that day and I put Teddy's certificates in his memory box, where they have stayed since that day.

Knowing what was wrong with Teddy gave a huge amount of relief in some ways; we knew something, finally. On the flipside of the coin it added to our pain and frustration. The doctors and geneticists were able to screen us both and tell us we didn't carry anything that could have been inherited by Teddy, which meant what had happened to him was a gene mutation. That's right, chance or luck – actually, bad luck. They think it was something that happened at the very second of conception, like any problem, condition or deformity does. Some people are born with an extra toe, some with one eye a different colour to the other, some have a condition that they will always have but can live with; Teddy's 'moment of conception' mutation meant that his condition was, in the doctor's words, non-life compatible. He was never going to make it on his own. They couldn't give us exact odds on it having happened to us, but they were the same as it having happened to anyone – completely random and unexpected. They think it was somewhere in the region of 250,000 to 1. Great, why us? The universe had felt, once more, decidedly unfair the day we found that out. I have to say, some days, the ones where grief lies a little heavier, it still feels exactly that – unfair.

★

The end of October finally came and so did the Warriors' meet up. They had all been so supportive during the time we had been finding out more about Teddy's illness, as had all our friends. I felt thankful that I could finally give other people answers when they asked me what had happened to Teddy.

We arranged to meet at a Pizza Express in Marylebone (not an #ad for all you Instagram lovers, just a bloody good pizza at a reasonable price!). I was so nervous, for so many reasons; mainly because I had to travel into London and manage my soaring anxieties without losing my shit on the journey. My parents were so worried about me that they insisted I got a taxi from Waterloo. Naturally the traffic was awful, a standard

Friday in London. I thought my heart was going to explode out of my chest with nerves and anxiety.

I walked into the restaurant and went downstairs. It was such a weird feeling. I felt like I had met these girls before, they were my friends, I knew pretty much everything about them; but the truth was, they had lived in my phone until that moment. I was (almost) the last one there, and I was met by a table of smiling faces, welcoming hugs and instant chatter; like we had been friends for years. It felt *so* wonderful to finally meet these women – to share stories of our babies, face to face, and to be able to call them friends in real life, not just Instagram/phone life, you know? The afternoon flew by and soon we had to say goodbye. I can remember coming away feeling so happy, so full of love for Teddy, and finally like I had actual friends who got it; because, sadly, they really did.

★

We are nearly two years on from that date now and, as I write this, those ladies are still firmly in my life. The chit-chat and banter on WhatsApp remains the same, as does the support they provide me. We call the babies 'The Gang' and take it in turns to write all of their names together in the sand whenever any of us find ourselves on a beach – that gang are well travelled now, I must say! We often joke about them being up in the sky having a rave, and how they watch over us. We all share the same optimism, the same hope that our lives will be filled with laughter again.

Some of the group have been blessed with more babies; precious rainbows that fill all of our lives with even more hope of better days to come. Although, understandably, those pregnancies have come with a new set of worries and anxieties to manage for each of them; losing a baby will do that to you. We are the ones who understand that, who don't immediately shriek congratulations at the first talk of pregnancy or congratulate them on being a 'first-time mum', because we understand that they aren't. It's just a new narrative of motherhood for them. It's a complicated path we have all embarked on, but one we are lucky enough to have each other for. The meet-ups continue, the celebration of our babies' birthdays are acknowledged, and we will continue to help and guide each other through this; for as long as it takes.

Sometimes you just don't know what's around the corner, or where the next decision might lead you. It's that 'sliding doors' moment that we all know can take us from one new reality to a completely opposite one. All I know is that I am glad that Michelle's photo stopped me in my tracks that day, I am glad I had the strength to actually reach out and say it had happened to me too, and I am eternally grateful that I found those women, because they saved me. It may be the club that no one wants to be in, but let's face it, if you've just become a fully paid-up member, you may as well have a bloody laugh now that you're in it and surround yourself with people who make the journey that little bit easier.

To the Warriors, I love you all.

Chapter 12

The Darkness
and the Dawn

WE LOST OUR SECOND BABY DUE TO MEDICAL
COMPLICATIONS AT ALMOST 15 WEEKS' GESTATION IN
JANUARY 2017. It was our longed-for rainbow baby –
a baby born after pregnancy loss, stillbirth or neonatal
death. The rainbow after the storm. It wasn't meant
to be, and it was a huge emotional and physical set-
back for me in my recovery. I was at a point where
I was starting to think that the universe was playing
some huge and unimaginably cruel trick on me; that
I would never bring a baby home. I had been slowly
starting to crawl out of the depths of grief over those
eight months and this had shoved me right back down
to the bottom of that lonely pit. So many of my friends

were pregnant again; I felt that I was the only one for whom it would never be so simple.

★

After nearly a year away from my job on maternity leave, I finally gave my notice in in March 2017 – breathing out a huge sigh of relief and even more of that pent-up anxiety! Not going back to my job was a huge decision, and not one that I took at all lightly. The decision-making process was all-consuming, and I can tell you that it kept me awake many nights worrying about exactly what I would be throwing away. After a particularly difficult Christmas and an equally bad start to January 2017, it dawned on me that there wasn't *really* a choice at all. The answer was already in me – I wasn't actually *able* to go back to my career.

As much as I could have tried, could have pushed myself to try and be the old me – be competitive, work to targets, appear confident and concise in client meetings – the truth is I *couldn't* do it. The thought of trying to do it brought a tsunami of that crippling anxiety over me, as did facing all of those people in meetings who had merrily waved excited old me off on my maternity leave the previous year. I feared I'd end up being continually signed off unwell and taking a huge step back in my mental and physical wellness. I'd worked *so* hard to get myself back on track and navigate this new version of 'normal' after losing Teddy – it took *every* ounce of positivity and human spirit that I had (mostly that I didn't even know I had!) – and selfishly I couldn't let *anything* jeopardise that.

I had been so passionate about my career, so conscientious. Hitting targets and deadlines always gave me a buzz. After spending my entire career in the beauty and spa industry, it was all I had ever known. I've held some brilliant positions in some fantastic organisations, and I feel very lucky to have done so. (Don't get me wrong, it's not really luck, I've worked bloody hard to get and keep those jobs!) So in some ways turning my back on it all felt like utter madness.

I still feel a little as though I'm in mourning for my career, as if everything I had worked and stressed over didn't ever really matter. Of course, in comparison to losing Teddy, it doesn't. Everything that came before pales into insignificance when you face the pain of losing your child; anyone who has lost a child or loved one can tell you that. Telling the company I worked for that I wasn't coming back, that I *couldn't come* back, was very difficult indeed. Trying so hard to articulate *why* actually brought me to tears.

When I was doing it all, it was with so much fire in my belly and passion for what I believed in, and I suppose that I just couldn't believe in it anymore. The other fundamental problem with the job was the people I would have to face every day – the new people almost every day. The 'getting to know about you' conversations every single bloody day. I wasn't just sitting in an office with the same people who knew about Teddy and could have the conversation with once and do my best to try and get on with things. I would have to put myself through the pain of regurgitating the whole story on a daily basis.

I know (only too well) that many mothers would give *anything* not to go back to work after their maternity leave, and that they don't have a choice. Likewise, many can't wait to get back into the swing of things. I don't know which category I quite fall into: '*Would love to go back to my normal, old, trouble-free life and career, but I can't because my son died.*' Not *having* to go back to that life makes me feel lucky, very lucky indeed; but the circumstances in which this decision had to come about kind of takes the shine away from it, I must say.

Of course I realise that everyone is different. For some people going back to work, to their old life and colleagues and to 'normality', is a huge part of their healing process, but for me it just wasn't an option. I also realise that there are many people and mothers who have lost their babies who have no choice but to return to their job, and I feel incredibly fortunate, but also incredibly sad for them at the same time. I wish we were all given the time and space we need to breathe, and to stop; so that we can just feel the things we need to feel after loss and we can start to heal again. I shall always be eternally grateful to my wonderful husband for allowing me to do so, as he continues working hard at his job. Who knows, if my job had been a different one then perhaps I would have mustered the strength to go back. Perhaps I wouldn't be sitting here writing this.

⭐

When I began to write my blog, just eight months after Teddy had died, in many ways I felt like I was well and truly late to the party (as always). Most of the other Warrior Women had long since been writing, some of them since the very early days of losing their baby. For me though, although I wanted to connect with people, I couldn't quite muster the strength and I was terrified that no one would listen. I suppose I feared that in writing about Teddy I would be exposing myself to the same misunderstanding.

It took until January 2017 to realise that it was OK to write about Teddy in a way that was filled with happiness and light. I had also needed the time to get my words straight in my mind. Grief and post-pregnancy hormones had done funny things to me; I couldn't get a sentence out in the right order, let alone set about writing a blog that another person could make any sense of. I needed to be sure that I felt strong enough to articulate myself properly, as I wanted to help other people in the desperate situation I had found myself in eight months ago; at least I thought I did.

When I look back now I realise that the blog and the words that I wrote were as much for me as they were for anyone else. It was, in fact, a way of healing – a form of therapy. It was somewhere for me to place all of my thoughts and feelings and talk about Teddy in the way I wanted him to be remembered. I also realised, slowly, that I didn't really mind about other people's reactions to my writing or if they didn't agree, because this was our story and I could tell it as I was living it, without fear of judgement from others. That felt *so* good.

When my writing did begin to help others, I realised

Teddy's story had become so much more than just something that had touched our family. Almost daily, people wrote to me sharing their experiences and I felt so honoured that they wanted to do so with me. They always began with saying that they had taken the time to read Teddy's story, and each time it meant so much to me. I could see that the positivity was spreading; that these women, like me, didn't want to be confined to the baby loss message-boards or forums to talk about their children. They wanted to feel empowered to speak their child's name every day, and for the outside world to view them as a mother even though they didn't have any living children here to physically show that.

While we are on the subject of blogging, my blog specifically, I want to tell you more about *why*, why I started it. My main focus of the blog was to reach out to those who hadn't experienced baby loss – if I am honest, I was tired of just reading baby loss blogs aimed at a baby loss audience. To me, they were nothing more than people screaming at the top of their lungs, locked into the unfortunate echo chamber they had found themselves in. I truly believe that you don't go searching for a baby loss or miscarriage blog unless you *have* to, in which case the worst has already happened to you.

How are we supposed to educate people and open up the subject of baby loss to a world of people who don't know about it if we just make it sound as scary, unthinkable and utterly miserable as it is? Answer: we won't. How are we supposed to get friends and families of those who have been affected by the loss of their baby to gain an understanding of what those people are going through, if the blogs in which those subjects are covered are only aimed at the people it's only actually happened to? Answer: we won't. Are you seeing what the fundamental problem is here? I could see it and I understood full well that there was a reason I didn't really know about stillbirth or neonatal death until Teddy had actually died and it was too fucking late for us. *No one was really talking about it!*

Teddy is my son, a part of our family and therefore included in all of my other passions in life. I wanted to create a place that allowed me to talk about *everything* that I loved; home, fashion, family and everything in between. Just because Teddy had died, I was not about to see his story swept off into a darkened corner of the internet because it didn't fit the perfect pixels that people wanted to see on Instagram. This is my life, *my* reality, and I am not about to hide it from anyone. If Teddy were here, if he were alive, would I have started a separate blog for him or an Instagram page all of his own away from the goings on of my 'normal' life? No, absolutely not. (Also, what new mum has time for that?!)

Even now, I sometimes find that when I post a new photo of Teddy and a caption that relates to his passing, there is usually a number of followers for whom the penny drops about my not-so-perfect life and they click the unfollow button as swiftly as their desperate thumbs will allow them. Does it bother me? Only that we live in a world that seems to strive for perfection so desperately through the observation of other people's tiny squares of life in our phones, that when the truth and reality of *real* life hits us, we can't quite handle it. Do I want people following me or reading my blog who can't see the beauty in those photos of Teddy, or understand that he made me a mother? Not one bit.

I try to write about Teddy with passion and with an eternal optimism that better days are set to come for our family. I have found that this has led to an incredible reaction from people who are invested in our story and not scared of what has happened. I hope it has allowed more people to look in through the glass onto a life that has been touched by child loss and bring them as close as is possible to understanding what it might feel like to experience something like that, and how you might look to carry on. If I am honest, if it is doing that, then in my eyes it has well and truly served its purpose, as it means that more people will be able to say or do the right thing when they encounter someone who has lost a child. I feel like that could be Teddy's real legacy, not just the fundraising – ensuring people in everyday society are better equipped to deal with the subject of child loss because they have taken the time to learn Teddy's story. What a wonderful legacy that would be.

Believe me when I say that, two years on, we are still so sad; but I think we wear our sadness rather well, especially in the outside world. I mean, people could actually be fooled into thinking I was totally fine! I have just found that continually crying and feeling sorry for myself doesn't get me anywhere, and it makes me feel so much worse and usually results in a face that requires permanent sunglasses, much like the early days. Of course, I still cry (big, heavy tears), and we feel sad; but not all day, every day.

Remember, *grief doesn't last forever, but love does.* I think that is exactly what has shown to be so true in our case – we have allowed our lives and hearts to fill with so much love for Teddy, that it has started to wash much of the sadness of grief away. We love him *so* fiercely and we do our best to parent him, and that helps us feel a little less sad. I like to think that each day we become a little more hopeful and a little less desperate in our sadness although, some days, inevitably, that wave of grief catches us off-guard and temporarily stops us in our tracks again; and that's OK.

Some people have even been brazen enough to ask me, 'How are you so happy and how do you stay so positive?' I think those people might prefer it if I only wore black and cried in the corner for the rest of eternity, only then might they be able to understand me. Some days I feel like doing both, but I have just learned other ways in which to manage my grief and sadness so that those days are lessened and the happy has (slowly) started to overtake the sad once again. I think many people don't understand how you can get on with it; how you possibly set about rebuilding your life after losing a child. Like with anything else, you don't know it's possible until you are in it and until you have to.

People always say things like, 'You are so brave.' I know that when people say those four words to me they are simply expressing, in the only way they know how, that they don't quite know how they would react if they were faced with the loss of their firstborn child. Let me ask you this though, what do you ordinarily do when life throws something your way that you weren't anticipating? Something that is entirely out of your control? I can tell you now that you do deal with it – you might not like it, but you face it head on. Why? Because you *have* to.

What if people didn't think that facing it and being positive was the right thing to do? (Side note again here: when you've lost a baby, there definitely is no right or wrong reaction.) I was fearful that my writing would be misconstrued by those who thought my words should be filled with darkness and sadness for Teddy.

The blog has proven itself as the best way to channel my energy, and even my friends read it in an effort to try and understand what we had been living through and gauge an understanding of my thoughts and feelings a little better. I couldn't have hoped for anything more. Maybe one day my blog will evolve into something that talks about another narrative of motherhood, and not just that of a mother who has lost – I can only hope that is the case. For now, though, like this book, I hope it talks to those mums who feel like there is no parenting manual out there for them, the ones who feel like they've been kicked out of the club. To them I say, 'Welcome to the new club (I know, you didn't want to be here!), and *everyone* is welcome.'

I suppose that this book is the ultimate manifestation of me trying to channel that positivity and give it a place in the world. It's a culmination of the writing, fundraising and open, honest humour that have enabled me to carry on since Teddy died. Hell, I am not telling you to go out and write a book to make yourself feel better (I'll be honest, I never imagined I'd write one, and it turns out that it's quite a lengthy process!), I am simply saying this: do what makes *you* feel better.

Chapter 13

Let's Do This

I THINK THERE COMES A MOMENT AFTER ANY UNEXPECTED EVENT IN A PERSON'S LIFE, WHEN THE REALITY FINALLY SETS IN THAT THIS IS THE HAND OF CARDS THAT YOU HAVE BEEN DEALT. However crappy those cards may seem, you realise you need to try your hardest to make the best of your situation. I have never been one to wallow for long, at least I try hard not to. That's not to say that I don't *feel* sad, of *course* I do. Even now, as we approach two years since Teddy died, I feel a sadness that is with me always because he is not here. I trust myself not to let that sadness override all that I do have in my life though – I would never want it to. As Nico had said just days after Teddy had died,

'We won't ever let this define us. He will be the reason we do, never the reason we don't.' Essentially, we were not about to curl into a ball and let the universe win on this one; we were going to do something positive in the wake of this disaster, anything that we could to make it hurt less.

I do wonder if my reaction would have been quite the same had I not been fortunate enough to have such a wonderful and supportive husband, the security of a happy marriage, and a loving family around us. I know that isn't the situation for everyone; but I do hope that everyone has someone in their life that tells them that they still *can* move forward.

I had started the JustGiving page just a week after Teddy had died as our way of telling the world what had happened and to try and do something, anything, positive in those early weeks. A two birds with one stone tactic, if you like. I became addicted to watching that fundraising total go up, it was mind blowing, I simply couldn't believe people's willingness to donate. All I kept thinking was what a huge difference that money would make to the care of sick babies in that unit.

As the weeks went by, a few friends asked, 'So when will you stop?' I didn't have an answer. The page could just keep going, I supposed. I was sure there was a time that would come where interest would dwindle and we would stop fundraising, but as 2016 rolled on, money *still* seemed to drop into the fund bit by bit. I always kept an eye on the total and found that the more I shared Teddy's story on my Instagram page, the more funds were raised. The odd five pounds here and there were really adding up.

When I started my blog, I knew that the fundraising needed to be front and centre of my writing. There was no point in raising awareness if people weren't then able to feel as though they might help in some way. Not help me, but help another family from leaving the hospital without their baby because, for me, that was all this was about. I think if you ask any parent who has lost a baby what they would wish for (apart from the obvious – that it hadn't happened in the bloody first place), it would be that no one else ever had to experience that pain, that *no* other family had to leave a hospital broken-hearted. That was what the fundraising had become: prevention over cure. I didn't *want* to be writing to all of these parents who had just lost their babies, because I never wanted for it to have happened to them in the first place. As far as I am concerned, the fundraising will continue for as long as it takes.

By February 2017 I had decided we would aim to raise £20,000 by Teddy's first birthday in May. We were already at nearly £16,000, so I hoped it was possible. The blog had been gaining some real momentum, with so many other bereaved parents and their families getting in touch with me.

What struck me the most though was how my writing had started to speak to people outside the world of child loss. That had been my aim, to open up that conversation to a much wider audience, not just those who were looking for it because the worst had already happened to them. People began to follow me on Instagram or read the blog who had never experienced child loss, but they wanted to *try* and understand it, and they were willing to talk about it. I finally felt as though I was making a real difference; people weren't scared of the subject, and it meant they also wanted to help spread the message even further.

I was contacted by a few other Instagram accounts who said they wanted to try and help me raise money and to hit the target I had set for Teddy's birthday, and what they began was like nothing I had ever anticipated. We began to use the hashtag #TeddysLegacy on all of the posts and, just like that, the word spread. People were donating, they were buying products from Instasellers who in turn made a donation to Teddy's fund. People began to contact me from all over the world saying that they wanted to help us raise more funds; I was astounded by their generosity and how we were able to connect with so many people. What I also found was that a theme began to show – their messages always began 'My sister', 'My mum', 'My friend'. Too many people knew someone who had been affected by child loss.

Why was this a subject that no one ever seemed to talk about, if it was happening all around us? Why had it taken me 32 years of my life and the death of my son before I realised this was the case? Again, it seems to come down to what our brains will often allow us to engage in; some subjects just seem too sad, too off-limits, *too* unthinkable. By writing about Teddy I was opening up conversations for people; new ones, and sometimes ones from many years ago that they needed to re-visit in order to allow those wounds to heal. The stories I have heard never cease to touch me or make me wish even harder that so many families weren't affected by this in their lifetime. I suppose once we have common ground, something that bonds us tightly like the loss of a child, we all begin to pull together in the same direction, and that direction became raising more money for the NICU which had tried to save Teddy.

★

I had kept in constant contact with the NICU since Teddy had died, as the paediatricians were working with genetics doctors to give us more answers about Teddy's condition. (They are still working on this, two years on.) I hadn't stepped foot in that unit again. I truly didn't know if I *could*. In April 2017 that changed, as I received an email inviting us to a re-launch of the unit's charity fund. I wanted to go *so* badly, to see the doctors and nurses, and to see the piece of equipment we had already been able to buy for the unit (co-funded by another family who had also been raising funds). We had been able to buy a brain monitor, like the one Teddy had been wired up to when he was poorly. It meant that they could treat another sick baby, and so fewer babies would be sent to another hospital if they became unwell like Teddy. I was thrilled and so very proud of what we had been able to achieve for them already. I was desperate to see it, so I could see all of our fundraising realised in something tangible that would actually make a difference to people's lives.

I accepted the invitation to the event, but I won't

lie – I was terrified of going back there. When the day came I don't think I realised the enormity of it until it was too late, and we were actually there. I thought it would be easy, a joyful event where we got to celebrate all we had done for Teddy as his parents. When we first arrived at the NICU, I got a sense of the huge difference our fundraising has already made. I was so happy to be able to tell them that it was still continuing, and that it would continue for a long time yet.

Walking back into that unit actually took every ounce of strength that I had; I can only describe many of the emotions as similar to walking back into flashbacks from a vivid nightmare. It didn't occur to me until we were in the lift on the way up to the unit that the last time I had been there was the evening of 19th May 2016, the evening Teddy had just died, when we were walking out of there with our hospital bags, but not with him. That wave of emotion came back to me with such intensity, I wasn't prepared. I felt like I had to walk along the corridor to look through the glass into the first room of the unit; the room where Teddy had been. As I stood there I stared intensely at 'his' corner, a place where he had been, where he had actually existed. As I stared, I felt strangely close to him. I felt as though he had given me the strength to walk back through those doors, to remind me why we were there, remind me of his purpose.

We had been asked to choose words for a plaque to go on the machine, so that other parents could see it had been donated in Teddy's memory. We decided upon words from one of Nico's favourite songs by Ben Howard:

> Donated by the friends and family of Teddy Wright, in his loving memory.
> Keep your head up, keep your heart strong.

Our target was smashed by his birthday. I couldn't believe it – we had raised over £22,000, in just a year, for the unit. After feeling that intense pride in all that we had achieved in Teddy's name in just a year, I knew the fundraising had to carry on.

I thought it would stop there but, as the blog grew, so did the fundraising projects we began to work on with sellers, makers and independent businesses. All through the power of social media – it was incredible! As I write this now, just nine months on from that date in the hospital, we have raised a total of over £50,000; by the time you read this, *who knows?* It has made me realise that anything can be possible in the wake of a tragedy, no matter how hopeless and helpless you feel at the time.

My husband and his friends are less than 90 days away from a charity cycle ride that will mark Teddy's second birthday and will see them cycling across France for seven days. There seems to be no end to people's willingness to help us raise funds in Teddy's name, and it makes me so proud. This has become our way of parenting him. It means I can use his name as part of a positive force, a force for good. Each time we run another raffle or someone approaches me to see if they could donate to the NICU, that's me being a parent to my son. I'll keep going, too. Even if we are lucky enough to be blessed with a healthy, living sibling for Teddy, I have promised myself that I will try my hardest to keep the fundraising going and keep including it as part of our family life.

My writing serves the same purpose. Sharing Teddy's name and his story enables others to feel like they can talk and share too. The more I talk about him and write about him, the more it enables me to connect with him as a mother, as his mother. That feels like a way of parenting, too.

Chapter 14

Please, Just Say His Name

IT BECAME SO APPARENT TO ME IN THE WAKE OF TEDDY'S DEATH THAT SO MANY PEOPLE STRUGGLED TO SAY HIS NAME OUT LOUD. I am not sure if it's because they found it too painful themselves, or if they deemed it might be too painful for me to hear it; a reminder of what we had lost. In the early days after his death it was only our family who had to face us and I think we all taught each other very early on that just ripping off the plaster and saying his name out loud as often as we could seemed the best way for us all to come to terms with what had happened.

'What had happened' – that term makes me shudder by itself, because it represents the unspeakable. So many people addressed Teddy's death as 'What you've been through' or 'After what happened to you'. It was so rare in the weeks after he passed to actually hear someone say, 'Teddy died.' That really got to me because, let's face it, that's exactly what had happened. Sadly, I think society's ingrained behaviour of not speaking about the death of a baby because it is too painful had rubbed off onto so many of the people we knew. Which left us as the ones who had to speak up. If we weren't prepared to say it, then it would seem that no one would, and I didn't want Teddy to become some kind of unspeakable event.

Even the letter that I received from the obstetrician at the hospital made me inclined to believe that people weren't going to accept Teddy as a person, that they wouldn't use his name. The week after he had died I received a phone call from the obstetrician's secretary asking me if I wanted to make a further appointment to discuss the delivery of my baby. In that moment I wanted the ground to swallow me up: she didn't know. I stumbled and stuttered to find the right words and eventually blurted out, 'I had my baby, last week, and he. . .he died.'

Now it was her that wanted the ground to do its thing and allow her to disappear from the other end of that phone call. The silence on the end of the phone deafened me. 'I am so, so sorry. I didn't have those notes here. I should never have called you, I didn't mean to upset you.'

The phone call swiftly ended and I sat stunned, trying to figure out who felt worse out of the two of us. What baffled me next was the follow-up letter. It arrived a few days later when the secretary must have explained to the obstetrician that she had committed the crime of breaking Rule 101 of the NHS: don't ring the lady whose baby has just died and ask her to come in to discuss delivery of a living baby.

The letter read, 'I am very sorry to hear about the unfortunate outcome of your pregnancy. . .' Not that my son has been born and had died, not that I had just lost my firstborn child – no, Teddy had apparently become my 'unfortunate outcome'. Teddy had become a nameless, faceless child, not just a dead one.

Teddy wasn't an 'outcome' or a sad event, he was a person; my son. I wanted to rip the letter up into a thousand pieces and throw it out of the window. It made me so angry that this man didn't recognise my son as a person. I didn't rip it up, though. I waited until I saw him for a follow-up appointment some weeks later and took it with me. Let's just say that I think he'll most likely re-think his use of wording in the future should a similar situation arise. All I wanted to be sure of was that no other mother would ever have to open a letter again that made them feel how I was made to feel. No one should *ever* be made to feel like that.

There was a situation when talking to a well-meaning friend that made me feel almost as bad, like no one would ever really see Teddy as my child. It came after we had been given his diagnosis as to why he was so poorly and why he died. During that time, I was doing my best to explain to our family and friends what Teddy's condition had meant for him. It was at that point when one friend made a comment, one she probably didn't even realise she was making and didn't have an idea of its impact upon me as Teddy's mother. She asked, 'I don't understand why your body worked so hard to keep him alive? You would think a pregnancy like that, with a baby that wasn't going to live, would just have resulted in a miscarriage much earlier?'

What I heard, of course, was, 'Your son shouldn't have been born, you should have had a miscarriage.' Those words burnt into me and hurt so much. I know she was just trying to make sense of what had happened, trying in some way to make me feel less guilty, but the outcome of that remark was the exact opposite. I wanted to tell her why my motherhood was worth as much as hers, why her words hurt me so much; but I was at a time in my life when I felt so fragile, so broken, I couldn't muster the strength to tell her how those words broke me that little bit more.

Of course people say things they don't mean in the wake of something shocking. I just wanted people to be a little bit more mindful and a little bit more understanding that I had given birth to a baby, full term, and then he had died. I knew that if I wanted people's acceptance, to be seen as a mother, then I was going to have to work a lot harder to get there.

People began to often address us with that familiar sympathetic head tilt (they still do) when talking about 'What we had been through'. Some failed to even say anything, just the tilt, perhaps with a shrug of the shoulders and a pained sympathetic smile. Now generally The Sympathetic Head Tilt comes hand in hand with the Benchmark of Shit (see Chapter nine) and can only be performed when people feel so utterly sorry for your circumstances that they really don't know what to say. It's when they know what's happened and they are approaching you for the first time since 'the event'. (Nico and I joke about this now

– I see it far less these days, but when I see it coming I do try not to chuckle to myself.)

It started to make me feel so sad that no one felt they could mention Teddy for fear of upsetting me. I'm not sure if it was a conscious decision to take matters into my own hands, or whether it kind of just happened over the weeks that followed his death, but I found myself saying the words 'When Teddy died' or 'When I was pregnant with Teddy' or 'The day Teddy was born' on repeat when I spoke to people. Each time it was like ripping off that painful plaster again, and again, trying to hammer it home to my subconscious the truly painful reality that our son had died. I recall seeing the shock in people's eyes, watching them wince ever so slightly as the words left my mouth. I am not sure who was more shocked when I said it, them or me. Sometimes I would say it aloud and think to myself what a sad story. Then I would remember it wasn't a story at all, but what had happened to us.

The other reason I think many people struggled to talk about Teddy, to say his name and recognise him as a person who had existed, was because they never got to actually meet him. They didn't see him or hold him; he was just a photograph of someone who had existed for such a short time in the grand scheme of life. His little soul danced into this earth and fluttered out again, just like that. I didn't want him to be 'just a photograph'. I needed him to be remembered as Teddy; a member of our family. When we meet someone, we remember the things about them, the way they smiled or the sound of their voice. People didn't have any of those tangible things of Teddy's to hold on to. All they had were our photos and our stories about his short time with us, which meant we had to try that little bit harder to bring those memories to life when we spoke so that people felt close to him.

As my closest friends began to talk about him and say his name, they would do so tentatively, like they were just trying it to see how it sounded out loud. I noticed their voices dipped in volume as those two syllables of his name began to creep into their conversation. I didn't care how quietly they were saying it. Or how weird it may have felt for them at first. All I could think was that my goal had been achieved – I said his name so often that they had begun to feel empowered enough to do the same. It was as though they could see that hearing his name aloud brought a smile to my face, one that represented the glow of a new mother; not the hurt and pain that his death had brought upon us.

I heard this phrase after Teddy died: you will learn

to feel the love more than the loss. For me, that's exactly what saying his name aloud was enabling us to do. By hearing it, normalising it and acknowledging his existence, we were filling that cavernous space of loss with love, so much love. Each time someone said his name or wrote it in a card, it filled that hole a little more. That was what I wanted to feel, especially after the early months of grief and loss had passed. I didn't want to live out the rest of my days in that murky bubble of grief and shock, I wanted to immerse myself in that love that we had for Teddy and start to do positive things in his name.

Writing his name down became a new hobby of mine. At first it was in letters to him in my notebook, but then it became anywhere I could – in the condensation of windows, in the sand of our favourite beaches, anywhere that made him feel that little bit closer. I would write it down in different ways in my notebook, lines and lines of just 'Teddy'. I would find myself wondering how he would have written it when he got old enough to write; would he have big swirly writing like mine, or my husband's less glamorous 'spider writing'? (I obviously hoped that it wasn't the latter!)

There were always safe places I could find to write

his name. The beach was my absolute favourite. I will never ever tire of seeing those five letters in the sand, even though Boris does his best to dig them up as I write them! As I said in Chapter 11, the Warriors all made a habit of writing names in the sand, we still do. There is something about seeing all of the babies' names together that warms my heart; to me it makes it feel like Teddy isn't lonely and that I shouldn't be scared for him. I take so much comfort in seeing his name surrounded by others, but at the same time it always saddens me to see them all there together. I think it's facing the reality of knowing that all of them are gone; it just seems too cruel, too impossible.

Their names have been all over the world now, but for me my favourite place to see Teddy's name will always be Constantine Bay. That beautiful place means so much to us, and seeing his name there just makes him feel so much closer. Sometimes I see other people walk by and read it as they pass us. I wonder if they wonder who Teddy is or if one day they might ask us? Sometimes I get the urge to shout at them as they pass and I see them looking, '*He's my son.*' But, for now, just knowing that more people get to see those five letters is enough for me.

I found it nearly impossible to decide what to do when it came to signing cards from us – should I include Teddy's name? Or was that too weird? I mean he *was* here, he *is* part of our family, but he was never *really* here, you know, long-term. It was such uncharted territory for us as a family, such a minefield; I knew there wasn't a wrong or right answer in how to deal with it, and I didn't want to upset anyone.

When our first Christmas without Teddy was upon us, I knew I would have to make some kind of decision on how I was going to acknowledge him. I was actually so scared about the prospect of writing Christmas cards and not writing his name in them that I decided to make a donation to a baby-loss charity in Teddy's name, to the value of what I would usually spend on cards and postage. I went on to social media to explain to everyone what I was doing. It was partly because we were only just six months on from losing him, but also because I couldn't cope with not seeing his name in those cards or writing it and then people thinking I had totally lost the plot.

I was off the hook from that particular task, and feeling rather smug that I had thought of a way to escape it, but there were still a few cards to write, ones to family and our very closest friends. I wanted to thank them all for being there for us through what had been the most difficult year of our lives.

After much deliberation I settled on a little 'T' inside a hand drawn star, just to the top right corner of our names. It made me feel like I had included Teddy. I know it might not suit everyone, but it felt right for us, and I have continued doing it to this day. Every time I write a card and put that little 'T' in it, it makes me feel proud that we are continuing to include Teddy in our family story. I never want that 'T' to disappear.

I think my love of writing Teddy's name was definitely what inspired me to write and share with others. I wanted to show people how healing it could be to just 'say it out loud', and to make them realise that there should be no shame associated with that. I also find myself writing those words again, over and over, 'When Teddy died.' It was like a kind of therapy for me, I suppose, seeing them there in black and white.

The first time I typed those words in a blog post I recall the burning in my eyes, that familiar feeling welling up ready to let those hot, heavy tears flow down my cheeks again. It was that reality check, the one that made me read it over, again and again, until I understood the impact of its meaning. Teddy had died.

There was something so cathartic about writing and sharing in those first months of the blog, that I found my words and feelings just came flowing out so easily. I never found any trouble in finding the 'right' thing to say when talking about my feelings that surrounded losing Teddy; I guess I was very lucky in that respect. I had given myself enough time to get those feelings straight in my head and now I was in a position to write those words.

The most impactful thing for me started when people began to write them back. Comments and emails that started with 'My daughter died'. Some even said things like 'I don't think I have ever written that before' or 'I have never told anyone I felt like that as I don't know who to share with.' It made me feel like the pain I had felt writing those three words 'When Teddy died' had been so worth it. It meant other people could say them too.

I don't think I understood the magnitude of what it would mean to just say those things, out loud, with an air of ease and nonchalance (not that inwardly I felt either of those things) – that it would help other bereaved mothers to talk, and to acknowledge their babies out loud; some who had never done so in decades. When I realised the enormity of that effect,

I knew it was the right thing to keep on writing and saying those three words.

★

Society still has a long way to go when it comes to talking about child death in an everyday conversation. When someone says, 'Do you have any children?' I usually have to decide in a moment whether I am going to share Teddy with them or not. I have to decide whether my heart is strong enough that day to say his name aloud and tell them that he died without the risk of bursting into tears. Usually because I don't want to cry in front of a stranger, but also because I don't want them to think they have upset me, or that having to talk about Teddy has upset me. Talking about Teddy and saying his name never upsets me, but sometimes in that moment when I have to play back the reality that we lost him, that's when I crack, and I can't hold back the tears.

It doesn't happen every time now, but it does still happen and I have to be prepared for it. The problem I think we have is that 'So, do you have any children?' or 'Is this your first pregnancy?' is such a commonplace question, one we would regard as casual chit-chat, but we don't really know the impact it could have on the person we are speaking to. We don't realise we might be putting them in a position that means they might have to share their story with us and give us a little piece of their heart.

I have had so many mixed reactions from people when I have told them about Teddy. My answer varies, but I tend to go along the lines of, 'Yes, I have a son, Teddy, but he only lived for three days and sadly never made it home with us.' It has taken me almost two years to practise that answer; saying it to myself at home so that I might be well-practised enough not to cry when I actually have to use it as my answer to a question from a real person. The first reaction, without a doubt, is always, 'Oh, I am *so* sorry.' People are always sorry, that's very British I think, we just can't help ourselves. I think it's a natural reaction and it's what we are almost trained to say as the reaction to the news of anyone passing away.

The bit that always troubles me, though, is what comes next, or should I say what doesn't come next? It is people's inability to take the conversation on from there, to say something (anything?) else. The awkwardness just kind of hangs there in the air, waiting for me to say something else about it, or for a complete U-turn in conversation to take place.

The way I see it is if someone's grandparent dies, we always start with the 'I'm so sorry', but then we usually follow it up with 'How old was he?' or 'Was she ill?' I think that's because we are so much more comfortable with talking about death, with discussing the subject of someone's passing in that little bit more detail, as long as that death doesn't defy the natural order of things. Sadly, Teddy's does. A mother should never lose her baby before she loses her own life; that's not how it is meant to be. Teddy going before me defies the natural order of how we expect life to pan out – its unfathomable and unspeakable – and so we find ourselves shocked into submission when it comes to addressing it in everyday conversation.

For that reason, I usually find that 'I am so sorry' is swiftly followed up by a passing comment about the weather that week, just to fill the air with noise rather than us both suffer the weight of the awkwardness that hangs in the air so heavily. All the while I find myself feeling as though I needlessly gave a little piece of my heart, and of my motherhood, to a stranger who couldn't even find it in themselves to ask another detail about my son. I have no doubt that it will take some time before we are able to iron out these conversational creases that society has engrained into the fabric of our conversations. I know it will be a while before someone says 'So, why did he die?' or 'Was your pregnancy full term?' as a knee jerk reaction to the news that my baby died, but I feel as though we are getting there. Slowly.

I hope that if we are lucky enough to have more children that they will speak his name confidently, that they will tell their friends that they have a brother who isn't here, one who lives in their hearts and through them. I hope that society will come to accept that all families are not the 2.4 children, happily-ever-after vision that we carve out for ourselves at a young age (at least I did), and that sometimes the answer to 'Do you have any children?' can be a little more complex than we are expecting.

I think my ability to say Teddy's name more often and more openly in social situations and through writing about him definitely contributes to my way of parenting him without him physically being here. It's a funny one that, trying to be a parent, when your child isn't here for anyone to see. As I have said before, I won't let the lack of Teddy's physical presence from this world be a path to my motherhood, or Nico's fatherhood, being simply erased. We are first-time parents just like any others. OK, so we don't have the dirty nappies or the sleep deprivation, but we are learning to navigate a new path of the unknown.

We are trying to connect with other parents who have gone through the same and are also just making it up as they go along. We are still parents. I feel the need to parent him in every single little way that I can, and I hate to miss out on any opportunities of doing so; whether that is by raising money in his name, bringing him into conversation, or indeed going the whole hog (as my husband would probably argue, I always tend to do that!) and writing an entire book about Teddy. It makes me feel like I am mothering him, like I am still able to connect with him, and I think it helps me quash any of the feelings I have around the fact that I wasn't able to save him, that no one was.

I think for us all to become comfortable and confident in saying the names of babies and young children who have passed away, this has to come from the parents themselves; we are the guides in this situation. Society will never know what's 'wrong' and what's 'right' unless we help them to recognise it. I have found myself far more inclined in the second year since Teddy died to say to people when I think they have spoken out of turn, or to encourage them to be more vocal when asking questions about Teddy and my feelings surrounding his loss. I don't ever want people to think they can't ask me, just like I didn't want my friends to think they couldn't say his name in those early days after he died.

So far, the mechanics of how people have dealt with and spoken about his death have been entirely led by my husband and me. We have been open and in turn other people have started to become so too. I think there just needs to be more of this, from every parent who has lost a child, in order to keep the momentum going. If we don't say their names, then we risk being silenced and having their stories driven back into those dark corners of the internet. We risk a new generation being brought up to think that the conversation ends at 'I'm so sorry'. When it really, *really* doesn't have to.

Please, just say his name. I do, and I *love* to hear it.

Chapter 15

Is This Forever?

I'LL START THIS CHAPTER WITH COMPLETE HONESTY: I THINK THIS FEELING *IS* FOREVER IN MANY WAYS. That's not to say I think I'll always cry when I say Teddy's name – some days I can say it out loud without so much as a flicker or burn of a tear threatening to make an appearance. What I mean is, losing a child *does* change you forever. Of course it does, I think any of us would be mad to think it didn't. There are some things that can never be undone, the effects of the event never reversed, and feeling that pain is most definitely one of them. As I've said before, it defies the natural order of how our lives are 'supposed' to play out. For me, it magnified the fragility of life and showed the real possibility of death. I think that losing Teddy took away much of my naivety when thinking about pregnancy and childbirth, something I miss so much and feel I have been robbed of.

I used to look at pregnant women and think, *Wow, how exciting*. Now I look and generally make a little wish that she gets to bring that baby home. Mad? Probably, but that's just one example of how losing my son has changed me forever. Anyone who has only ever had a healthy pregnancy that resulted in the birth of a healthy child will fully expect that to be the case when she sees someone who is expecting. What about if your only experience of pregnancy and birth is now filled with sadness and loss? I find it so hard to look at anyone who is pregnant and not worry for them, and I think that worry is perfectly justifiable given what I have experienced.

I never want anyone else to feel that loss, and I am so fearful, now that I know the statistics of what *can* happen, that it *might* happen to someone else. I am well aware that this makes me sound like the angel of death, and I promise that this is not where I am going with this – I am just trying to explain how my mind has begun to work since losing Teddy. I am most definitely not a sceptical person, I never have been, but I look at things in such a different light now. It's like having your eyes opened to the fact that anything is possible, and not necessarily in a good way. Most days I wish I could give that knowledge back, I wish I could just see the world as I did before, and then life would become so much easier again. Then I remember that I am trying to be grateful for everything that this path has taught me, so I just give myself a stern talking to and carry on looking at the world through this new lens. . .

Even on my most positive days I often get brought back down to earth with a bump. It dawns on me that being cautious and much more quietly optimistic is my new outlook. I am ever hopeful that things will be better, because they can't be any worse. I know that I am not quite 'myself' anymore. I don't know where 'old me' is hanging out these days, but I do miss her. She was carefree, positive and always had something funny to say to brighten up the days of others who were struggling, even if she was prone to taking the piss a bit too often! All of my friends always knew me as a joker, someone who would think of something funny to say even in the most desperate of times (oh jeez, I sound as though I am writing my own obituary here!).

Some days I wake up and I feel a bit like her; I feel like I could maybe do a full day at my old job or go to a big event without so much as a single pang of anxiety or panic. Then there are the other days, the ones when I remember why I feel *so* different now. The days when I feel desperate and I miss Teddy so much that it consumes me. I think those days are getting fewer, and when they come they don't feel as heavy in many ways. It makes me think that, eventually, they might even fade away altogether. Those are also the days that make me feel close to Teddy, as the more time that passes and the further away from us those dates of his birth and death become, the more I find myself hopelessly searching for ways to feel as though he and I are still connected. Those days when the grief consumes me are the reminder that he was here, that we are indeed connected; and it would seem that I love and hate those days in equal measure.

I always try my hardest to think about the positive changes in myself since Teddy died. I look at ways to try and see how far I have progressed since those earliest and darkest days of grief and shock. Let's face it, I couldn't even face my friends then and I was scared of stepping out of the bloody front door, so I would say we have come on in leaps and bounds since then, wouldn't you? I think that when you don't look at the extremes in that way, it's easy to think you haven't made any progress when actually you have. I mean, it's not going to happen overnight, but it *will* happen.

I never want my reflection upon how my feelings are evolving as time goes on to be perceived as wallowing, and sometimes I fear they might be. For anyone reading who's not lost a child, a sibling or someone significant in their life who was taken from this world far too early, you might find it very difficult to understand why the pain of something like that takes so long to dull and has such a huge impact on every aspect of a person's life. If you do know someone who is suffering as a result of a loss like that, be mindful that they most likely won't be bouncing back to their 'old self' anytime soon. That's not because they don't want to (trust me, I really do), but it's just not that simple.

Almost a year after Teddy had died, my mum was asked by a family member if I was OK because I 'didn't seem myself'. I know eleven months had passed, but really, was I supposed to be my old, chirpy self, just eleven months after my son had *died*? I think Mum, who has lived through every breath of this pain with us, was just as dumbfounded by this question as I was. I know that she did her very best to explain what we are living through, and that some days just getting up and facing the world is a huge achievement for us.

It just got me thinking, *Is this what everyone expects?* Am I supposed to just miraculously recover from the death of my son and act as if he had never existed? Well I won't, I don't want to. Perhaps, for that reason alone, I *do* want this to be forever. I felt like I was in mourning for the old me – I began looking through photographs and my social media and longing to look that happy again. I stared at a photo of me and Nico on West Wittering beach that we had taken the day after we had found out we were expecting Teddy. The sun was beaming on a late September day and we both looked so blissfully happy. I studied the details of our faces and tried to think back to that day and exactly how it had felt. I tried to put myself in that position again and fill my mind with that much hope and optimism. For a second, I almost got a flicker, but then my next thought is always of Teddy.

I could see around me that everyone was moving on with their lives and yet I was desperately trying to wade slowly though a year of 'firsts'. That first year felt like the world had decided to turn especially slowly just for us. That year, that should have been filled with milestone cards, gurgles and weaning, was instead filled with the dread each time a 'first' was on the horizon. First Christmas, first Mother's Day, my first birthday without my son. (The previous year I had been smugly 36 weeks' pregnant and posing for a birthday photo on a lounger in a spa, proudly showing my bump and grinning like the Cheshire cat.) I felt like I wanted to disappear on my next birthday, and I think that was because mine is less than a month before Teddy's, and we were building up to a crescendo of events that led to that ultimate one-year mark. One whole year of being parents without a baby to show the world. One whole year of living in what felt like a parallel universe, which was strangely starting to feel like home, as the memory of what life was like before became exactly that: a memory.

Getting through that first year felt like running a marathon (not that I have ever actually run in one, but Nico has run a few, so you know, I'll take that one by proxy). It was such a hard slog. It felt never-ending, and when we did eventually get through it I wanted to set off a confetti cannon of relief and yet also felt like nothing had changed. After that year mark passed though, I did feel distinctly lighter. It was a bit like that day of Teddy's funeral when Nico had said to me that we had come through the worst of it, that that was the worst we were ever going to feel. That year had to be the worst, the most difficult. There couldn't be another year like that, because we had already done the first of everything; it had to get easier from hereon in. I suppose that your senses harden to it over time and you get used to the pain, so you feel it a little less, you wear it a little better.

I find myself always looking for people who are further into loss than I am – months ahead, years ahead – trying to see if I can view my future ahead of me. Will I feel like that? Are they feeling better than me? I think it is my way of finding hope; a hope that it gets better from hereon in. When I hear from a parent who has lost a child many years before us, and they tell me that they are still here and that they are surviving and feeling happy, it fills me with exactly that same feeling. This goes back to the time shortly after Teddy had died and I was endlessly searching through what felt like the entire internet for a blog or a thread (or in fact anything) that spoke to me, that wasn't telling me how bad it was in this moment but how I *was* going to survive. For me, connecting with families who are much further along in their loss than we are brings that same feeling of optimism – those better days lie ahead.

I suppose it's no different than when your children are young and they aren't sleeping through the night, and it's an endless cycle of nappies and night feeds and then you see someone with older children and it looks like it gets easier as time goes by! It's that natural instinct of wanting to look ahead and think, 'OK, it won't be like this forever.' New parents want time to slow down as they want to cherish the moments they have with their little ones, and in many ways I feel like that too. Time feels as though it moves slowly, but then I am only moving slowly away from those moments when Teddy was with us. The reality is, of course, that time is an utter turd and none of us have any control over how it continues to hurtle ever onwards... So as much as I want to keep close to Teddy, I have to find other ways in which to do so. I always keep those families in the forefront of my mind, the ones who tell me that it's 'Going to be OK', because I know they are right because they have lived to tell the tale.

I don't know if it's ever possible for the 'old me' to make her comeback, no matter how much time passes. Do you know something else? In many ways I'm not even sure I would want to be completely my old self now. When you strip away all of the negative effects that losing Teddy has had on me (the anxiety, fatigue, the feeling of loneliness, random bursts of floods of tears), there are the great ones too. I think that having Teddy has changed me and losing him changed me even further. I'm more cautious than ever before, more of a thinker than I have ever been, and less of a planner – I really think all of us could do with a little less planning now and again, and a little more spontaneity! I used to be short-tempered, I'd even say quite fiery, and I used to let the little things *really* get at me – they just don't anymore.

Yes, Teddy died, he's not here, but having him has made my heart feel fuller than ever before. Becoming a parent has made me feel a kind of love I knew nothing about, and we've had to learn to 'parent him' as best we can without him physically being here. Sometimes that comes from just talking about him or raising awareness about his illness. Sometimes it comes in the form of fundraising. Many days it is merely me sitting in his room and talking to him, reminding him how very loved he is by his entire family.

I often wonder if Teddy had lived would I have changed in as many positive ways? I mean, I know the negative changes wouldn't have existed, but what about the positive: would I have gained those if he were here? I'm definitely a better listener, a friend who gives better advice and I hope a better wife, sister and daughter. I am far less judgemental, and I think more about what other people might be going through.

When we were trying for Teddy and I was so desperate to be pregnant, every pregnant person I saw immediately got under my skin, every social media announcement made me want to hurl my phone into another room. Since having Teddy and losing him, when I see a pregnant lady or someone with a pram I find myself looking at them and wondering. How long did it take her to get there? Has she had a miscarriage, or maybe even more than one? Did she have a long road of fertility treatment to get that baby in front of her? The chances are that 'no' might be the answer to all of those (we all know those fortunate women who seemed to be able to pop out babies as easily as shelling peas), but what if the answer to one of those is 'yes'? Who am I to judge someone else's situation simply by looking at them? I often wonder if I'd have thought that carefully about things if Teddy had been here. I doubt I'd have had time to.

Since becoming a mother I am somewhat of an emotional wreck, like many of us. I cry at an advert, at an episode of [insert name of *any* programme here] – I can't seem to help myself! It's as if I used to worry about letting those tears go, and now I have absolutely no inhibitions at all when it comes to having a good old cry. In fact, I usually feel a million times better when I do so I just let them flow freely. I know that happens to so many people after having children, but having Teddy and then losing him seems to have left me with a new-found vulnerability when it comes to my emotions. It's not uncommon for me to burst into tears, and it can take me by surprise (and it usually does). It probably worries some people or makes them think I am not dealing with losing Teddy, but for me I think it shows that I am not scared of those emotions and I don't mind who sees me crying. Sometimes there are also happy tears!

I know that as time passes, more people will begin to expect us to get back to our 'old selves', but I'm not sure how I go about telling them that's not going to happen. It sounds a little harsh. Even now I find myself answering the question, 'So, how are you feeling *now*?' –usually with emphasis on the word now being indicative of the amount of time that has passed since Teddy was born. Am I expected to have miraculously recovered and say, 'Oh yeah, that, I'm over it'? Wishful thinking on everyone's part, I think. I am really not sure what people expect me to say! Do I just tell the truth and respond with, 'My son died, and

I still think about him every day.' I mean, talk about killing the mood (again). I think that people need to hear that you're 'OK' and that you're coping, just so that they can feel a little better that they've been able to move on, even though they know that you will never. Sometimes I feel pressure to be happy or to just lie and say 'I'm fine'. (So British, no matter what the question is.) Then other days I feel the urge to remind people that the loss is still very much present in our lives, and always will be.

Teddy will always be our firstborn child, the one who didn't get to come home. No matter what happens, nothing changes that. No matter what changes as we move forward, one more child or *ten* more children, there will always be one missing. One less person around the dinner table, one less pair of wellies by the back door, one less 'Mum' being shouted as these metaphorical future children argue over the TV remote (or iPad, or whatever it is siblings will inevitably fight over in the next decade). *Always* one less. But he will always be loved and talked about, and we will carry his memory with us always too.

The 'new me' has learned to talk about him more confidently now, honour his memory in the ways she sees fit, and raise funds for other children in his name.

She is trying each day, not to be her old self, but to learn to love this new version; the one that has learned so much from these past two years. And do you know something? I think I'm starting to quite like her. . .

Chapter 16

Knowing
My Limits

I OFTEN WONDER WHETHER I SHOULD JUST START EVERY CONVERSATION WITH A STRANGER WITH, 'HI, I'M ELLE. My son Teddy died.' I mean, it might make things easier, right? You would get it 'out there' straight away, without it lurking in the back of your mind or waiting for the moment that person asked the inescapable question that means you just have to spill the truth and hope they won't run away for fear of having upset you. The truth is, I *can* talk about it now, I can say his name to strangers; I have made myself well practised at this art (without always bursting into tears too!). I also hope that I can talk about it in a way that makes the person listening begin to understand a little about the life you find yourself catapulted into after the loss of a child, and make them feel less afraid to ask more questions. After all, Teddy is my son, and I do want to talk about him.

In the early days, I can remember telling Nico that it was a bit like pinching yourself to feel the pain, to realise the reality of your circumstances. I felt as though if I purposefully did things and said aloud 'Teddy died', the pain of doing so would allow my subconscious to catch up on what had happened and thus allow each time to become that little bit easier. As I have said, initially I couldn't write those two words together, but I can now. In many ways I suppose I was right, it did seem easier the more I was brave enough to say it aloud; but the pain, the dull ache of emptiness, remains the same. How is this? I mean, surely if I just kept saying it, it wouldn't upset me, right? Wrong. I'll be the first to admit I was wrong. Yes, I can say it without physically bursting into tears, but the hollow feeling, the lurching of my stomach that tells my head and heart that something went so incredibly wrong remains very much intact. I am not sure if that will fade.

It's because of these feelings that I have learned to manage my limits when it comes to daily life and the events that inevitably occur along the way. Meeting new people, seeing old friends (the ones you haven't made time for since you were the 'old you' but you will have to see eventually), navigating events such as weddings and parties; all of these things have changed for me. I want to share a little about what I have learned along the way since Teddy died; from the early days, to the here and now.

These days, I tend to focus my energy and tactical planning on the bigger occasions. However, in the beginning, in the immediate weeks and months that followed his death, it was even the simplest of tasks that commanded my attention in order to find the best way to approach them. I read in, I think, a Sands leaflet, not long after Teddy had died, that often when people lose a newborn baby they start to shop in a different supermarket for fear of bumping into someone they know, or encountering a situation that reminds them of their pregnancy. This sounded mad when I read it, but began to ring entirely true to how my behaviour was changing. I did indeed change where I shopped; mainly for the fear of the chatty checkout ladies in our local Waitrose who had wanted to talk to me about my pregnancy throughout. How far gone was I? Boy or girl? Due date? Was it my first? (You know how it goes, all of the questions that complete strangers feel compelled to ask when you are sporting a bump.) I was of course initially over the moon to share the details of my anticipated arrival and engaged in conversation with each of them every time I shopped, but now the thought of stepping back into that supermarket made me feel physically sick.

When I think about it now, perhaps they wouldn't have even recognised me. What if they had, though? What if, on the one occasion I had stepped foot in there and dared to go ahead with trying to be the 'old me', that someone had politely and excitedly asked me if I had had my baby yet? There would be nowhere to hide and that thought terrified me; so up the road to Sainsbury's I went, seeking anonymity in the aisles.

It wasn't just the weekly shop that needed ninja style organisational skills to navigate in those early weeks. There were also daily dog walks to think about. Boris helped me so much during my recovery after Teddy died. He was my reason to leave the house, whether I liked it or not. Most days the thought of leaving the house filled me with absolute dread, so I would find myself mentally gearing up to it. All the while Boris would be trotting around my ankles looking up at me in the anticipation that we would indeed embark on our daily walk – there is nothing like a needy pug to give you the guilt trip you need to make sure you do something! I began to plan our walks early morning or late in the evening. Luckily as Teddy was born in May we were well into late spring and heading for the summer months, so both the mornings and evenings were conveniently light. I wore sunglasses at every opportunity on these walks (or indeed when leaving the house). This was for two reasons:

1) I felt as though I was disguising myself from the world.
2) If I did happen to bump into anyone then I could easily burst into tears behind them and the chance of them knowing the full extent of my upset was softened slightly. I felt it would be, anyway.

I can recall many walks when I did indeed bump into those friendly neighbours or people I had met when out with Boris when I was pregnant. These were the 'first encounters', and unlike the ones with friends that had been planned and navigated in a way to create the least awkwardness for both them and for me, these chance meetings with acquaintances were particularly tricky and upsetting to manage. Many chose to ignore that I was no longer the size of a small village, and as they didn't mention it, neither did I. Looking back, they must have known something had gone terribly wrong and had just chosen in that moment not to say anything for fear of upsetting me; or perhaps they just thought I had left my newborn baby at home with my husband when I walked the dog? It does seem strange not to mention it at all, but what I have learned is that human nature can be quite strange and shock does very odd things to people.

Of course, there were also the people who came hurriedly towards me with a beaming smile and a 'Soooo, what did you have?' only to be greeted by my dead-pan face and quivering lip before I either plucked up the courage to blurt out what had happened to Teddy, or (and this second version of events often happened) I opened my mouth to speak and no noise came out, not a peep. Instead I would just cry and stutter and they would get the gist before apologising (probably wishing the ground would just swallow them up even more than I wish it would me in that moment) and be on their way pretty quickly. Yep, nothing kills a conversation more than that topic, I can tell you.

I began carrying around a sense of guilt that my not-so-happy news would darken people's days. More and more I tried to walk Boris in new places or at quieter times. It was less risky and meant I could use the time to actually clear my mind, look around me, and start to be in each moment again without the guilt being wrapped around me like a blanket of shame.

I found new and exciting ways to seek anonymity. My lovely yoga instructor had been so supportive in the weeks that followed Teddy's death, and she gently encouraged me to return to a midweek, morning class, as most of its group members were older or middle aged, perhaps retired even. Other than the pleasantries exchanged at the start of each class there was no in-depth conversation, no 'So what do *you* do?' To this day, two years later, there are now only a handful of them who have discovered my blog and know about Teddy. The others don't know what I *do* or what my life is about, and I likewise for them. For the moment, it is just easier this way, as it enables me to feel safe and to feel no pressure or expectation in that environment. To feel fully as though I can enjoy the class without being 'the lady whose baby died'; instead I'm just Elle.

It's the little things like this that have enabled me to regain a sense of normality and a sense of myself, and I am not quite ready to be deprived of that just yet. Who knows, maybe one day I'll march in to class wearing a self-styled T-shirt that reads 'I'm Elle, my son died' and hand them a signed copy of this book. I doubt it, but the thought does make me smile. I have come to be very thankful for those classes, for the sanctuary they have provided, the strength they have given me and the way in which I was able to do something for myself again. They were the first real step to my new outlook, my new regime of self-care and self-preservation; the first real part of the 'new me' that I actually liked.

These early experiences were the foundation upon which I based my own theory about knowing my limits with what I could and couldn't navigate. Of course, in the early weeks we barely did anything; in the months that followed I think we had one social occasion (with our very closest friends, of which more later) in the calendar, and as the months crept on a few more things started to filter in. I couldn't plan ahead, it just wasn't a possibility for me; I had to take each day as it came. In many ways that is still true now. I used to relish making plans, having lots of things to look forward to in the calendar. After Teddy died I can remember people saying, 'Why don't you just get away from it all and go on an amazing holiday?'

I can just remember thinking, *why* would we want

to waste money going to a beautiful location just to sit and be miserable there instead of doing that at home? There wasn't any 'cheering up' that was going to happen, there was no miracle fix; most certainly not with a beach and a bit of vitamin D. Our impromptu mini-break to Cornwall had proven that this was going to take huge amounts of time, and I didn't want to rush it or end up creating a holiday of miserable memories where we just sat staring at each other's miserable faces. We made a promise to ourselves that when we began to find happiness again, we would go somewhere lovely on holiday, somewhere we could both enjoy and look forward to making some happy memories. For the moment, I just take things day-to-day most of the time, and that suits me just fine.

I find that some people are less understanding of the time that all of this has taken (is *still* taking) and of course there are the ones that will never 'get it', but there are always the friends that do. The wonderful friends that are with us on this ride to the new normal and who understand completely that these things take time. I love the fact that our friends haven't given up on us – not quite yet, at least! They still make sure that they invite us to everything, and always did, even in the early months. I can remember one of our good friends saying to me, 'Elle, I'll always invite you, even when I know you can't come yet. One day though you might feel like it and that will be lovely.' It's attitudes like that that enabled us to go at our own pace and have allowed me to have weeks when I can socialise and weeks when I can't.

Luckily, I can say now as I sit and write this chapter nearly two years after losing Teddy, that those good weeks where I *can* do things are starting to become much more frequent. I still get the days where I push myself too hard, do too much, or something that is out of my comfort zone again, and I always pay for it. I have just learned that if I do that then I need to give myself some recovery time, some quiet days at home that allow me to heal again. The crippling anxiety that I suffered from in the weeks that followed Teddy's death has softened now, but like much anxiety brought on by grief, it has led me to a new way of managing my activities and emotions so as to ensure that it never comes back like that.

Once the day-to-day tasks are out of the way and you've got first meetings, arranged or by chance, out of the way, you're just left with the big stuff, the 'events' in life. The big things in life still absolutely terrify me. If we have a party or a wedding coming up, then I know I need to allow myself lots of days at home in the lead-up to the event in order to feel strong and capable enough to face it. Weddings are the most difficult – seeing all the people you know, talking to the ones you don't. Bracing myself for the 'So, do you have any children?' question and then wanting to run and hide. Luckily, most we have been to so far have been relatively pain free, and again our friends who have invited us have been really mindful of positioning us among the people we know and who don't need to ask questions.

I have also managed one christening since losing Teddy – my best friend's son, to whom I was godmother. This was the event just three months after Teddy died, and I will be the first to say that I think it was too much for me to handle, too soon. Stepping into the church brought me to tears, talking to people had the very same effect. When the christening service was over I just sat in the pew and crumpled into tears; physically shaking with pain. It all felt so, so unfair; knowing that this would never be happening for Teddy. His one occasion in front of his family at the front of the church was both his first and last – his funeral service.

Of course, lots of people might be reading this and thinking 'Why on earth would you put yourself through the pain of a christening?' Well, my best friend had asked me to be a godmother shortly after her son was born, at the end of 2015. I was about 16 weeks' pregnant with Teddy and filled with the joy and excitement that any expectant mother should be. We chatted about how lovely it would be for them both to be so close in age (we didn't find out that Teddy was a boy, but that would have been pretty bloody perfect in hindsight if they had grown up together). Anyway, obviously I agreed – she is my best friend and it was a huge honour. After Teddy died she told me that I didn't have to be godmother if I wasn't up to it, or that they could always move the christening if it wasn't the right time.

My thoughts at that point were that there would *never* be a right time for me. Going to a christening or becoming a godparent to a young baby would always be painful for me, especially if I thought about it long enough in relation to the loss of our son. So I told her that I wanted to go ahead and do it; to be there for her, just as she had been there for me in recent months.

I am glad that I did. It was the first thing I did after Teddy died that I can honestly say I did for someone else, and didn't run away from the pain. Strangely it made me feel stronger and more capable to push myself to do more in the months that followed. It was a baptism for everyone else in that room, but a baptism of fire back into the real world for me. Once it was done it was done; and I felt better for it.

Now, I understand that this may not be the right approach for everyone, and I would hate to think of someone causing themselves unnecessary pain or suffering by thinking they must do the same; but it worked for me. I always find the build-up much worse than the actual occasion. Once I am there, at an occasion, I now find that I am OK. I think that's a case of having got all of the 'firsts' out of the way, the very painful events are over; so for me everything seems to have got much easier from there on in.

By 2017 I started to get into the swing of managing the social side of life again much better. Saying yes when I could, and no when I had to. My husband and I still get invites and say to each other, 'Do you think we can?' I am not sure how long that will last, perhaps forever. I have found myself getting much better at social events too, being more 'me' and less of a worrier about what might be said (or not said, it works both ways!). I'm also not scared to have a glass of wine these days; to kick back and actually try to enjoy life again. There was a time in the early months after Teddy died that this was very much not the case. I was riddled with guilt; and it's a guilt I definitely still carry with me now, although it has softened a little. Now this is a bit like the 'mum guilt' I read and hear mummy bloggers speaking about. You know, the one where they carry this constant layer of guilt on top of everything they do; because they are working, not working, doing too much of something, not doing enough of something – you know how it goes. I know from friends who have children that it's a very real emotion indeed. My 'mum guilt' is very different; and I think it's been there constantly since I embarked on my mission of attempting to get back into the swing of 'normal' (I hate that word) life. I feel *guilty* that I am happy, guilty that I am laughing, *guilty* that I am getting up and attempting to get on with my life, *guilty* that we want another baby, and ultimately *guilty* that it's all done without Teddy.

I've said so often that 'life goes on', whether we like it or not. The way I see it is, I had a choice: to 'Choose Life' (Yes, George!) again, or to simply shut the world out and sit in a darkened room reflecting for eternity on how cruel life had chosen to be to us. I can tell you that, as much as the early days of grief had beckoned me to do the latter, I decided I wasn't going to shut the world out; not ever. As I now try to stay true to that way of thinking, the guilt still engulfs me very often. I'm not sure if it will ever leave (I mean, I wish it would just piss off), or if this is just my life now? Can you feel guilty *forever*? Will I end my life feeling guilty that I lived the rest of my years out without Teddy and I actually enjoyed things and learned to laugh a few times along the way? I really, *really* hope not. For now, I have learned to live with the guilt, to simply manage and approach it, as I do with my anxiety. To try to understand *why* it's there and what the things are that might help to ease it a little and make me feel a little less, well, guilty I suppose.

One of the biggest changes I have made in my life since Teddy died up until this very day was get my work/life balance right. My ability to get up and go to work each day changed, completely – I just couldn't – and so I didn't.

Some days I *can* do it; I can get up, be an adult, do life, endure situations that are stressful and I don't so much as flinch at any of it. Other days... well other days I just about manage to take Boris on a walk at the beginning or end of the day in the quietest of locations. Those days, the ones where grief engulfs your being and pulls you down from your usual 'happy place', those are the days that wouldn't make doing my old job possible. How do you call your boss and say 'Sorry, I can't do life today'? I couldn't do that; it's not fair on me or on the company I worked for. I didn't want to be that person.

★

I believe (and yes, this is an absolute ton of cheese coming your way) the saying 'You are only one decision away from a completely different life' to be entirely true. If I hadn't decided at the start of 2017 that I would not be returning to my job, then undoubtedly I wouldn't have started to share my experiences with others by writing a blog. In turn I wouldn't have been afforded the opportunity to write guest posts on the established and brilliant blogs that I have done, and I most certainly wouldn't have been given the opportunity to write this book.

So yes, you *are* only one decision away from a completely, and utterly, different life. This isn't the life that I would have planned by any stretch of the imagination, but it is where I find myself now. All of these new adaptations I have made in my life are to be kinder to myself, and to make dealing with the reality of life after loss a little less painful. There are things

I am still yet to encounter too, and when I do I shall do my utmost to take those in my stride and navigate each event.

For me, the main thing I take away from everything since losing Teddy is that we are all *so* different. Much like that first encounter I had with the bereavement midwife, when I realised I was being expected to behave and to grieve in a certain way and I knew that wasn't *my* way. Just like my experiences in this chapter may not be the way that others choose to adapt after experiencing a loss. Making changes to help ourselves find a new way forward in our lives is so important after loss, however we might choose to do it. This is my motherhood, and I'm embracing it.

Chapter 17

Learning to Live Again

WHEN YOU ARE IN THE DEPTHS OF GRIEF YOU WISH THAT SOMEONE WOULD JUST COME AND PULL YOU UP FOR AIR; JUST A MOMENT'S RESPITE FROM THAT HEAVY, SUFFOCATING FEELING THAT TAKES OVER YOUR LIFE. That usually comes in the form of laughter or distraction; for me, in the early days, it was being able to laugh with friends and just 'be me' without the pressure of being the girl whose baby had just died. I wanted to laugh, to joke as I always had done, without being judged or it being assumed that I had 'got over it'. I wanted to just feel free for a moment. That grief, that all-encompassing powerful loss, is never further than a thought away, so you may as well just escape it in the small moments you can manage to, and fully embrace those moments.

It is now almost two years since losing Teddy. One of the things I have found we all seem to have in common when we experience the loss of a baby is that desire to 'feel better'. A number of women have written to me who have recently experienced the loss of a child, to simply ask, 'How did you do it? How did you start to feel happy again?' Lots of them want to know when it will happen for them, or what the magic formula is to find something that resembles their old life, the one before the heartbreak. I never pretend to have the answer, and I always tell people that we all grieve and recover differently. I do believe, however, that we are born with a certain amount of resolve as individuals and that some of us have the power to use our positivity in a time of darkness and helplessness to help ourselves overcome it. I count myself as incredibly lucky that I seem to have gained an abundance of both resolve and a positive mindset from my parents. Whether this was a case of nurture over nature, I am not quite sure. Nico is the same, and we knew that losing Teddy wasn't going to beat us. We knew we had to help ourselves to recover from this.

★

YOGA

I have already talked about how helpful I found yoga in the months after Teddy died. I still practise at home several times a week and attend classes. It has given me strength and positivity, eased my anxiety, and allowed me to start getting my usual confidence back. Yoga is great for fertility too – I didn't even know that when we had been trying for Teddy.

There are so many things I want to tell you about how much yoga helped me, but I am no expert. I know that it made me feel better, but I don't necessarily know why. I know that it made me feel more able to cope with the everyday things that life threw my way, but again, I am not sure how. Luckily, I do know someone who knows a thing or two about it all. Take it away, Louise!

What is yoga and how would you describe its power to someone who didn't know about it?

Yoga means 'union', joining together the body, mind and spirit. Yoga is an ever-evolving, rich and diverse living tradition, which originated in India, but now blends eastern and western influences.

It is a system for us to arrive in the present moment,

re-connect to our true nature, to experience inner peace. Yoga is not a religion, but is a spiritual practice, leading us to the realisation that we are connected to something greater than ourselves, whether you see that as a God, the Universe, Spirit, Higher Self or True Self – so that we may feel whole.

With the many diverse offerings of yoga, students should explore which practices work best for them personally. Hatha yoga classes explore yoga postures, breathing techniques, relaxation practices and meditation, all designed to deepen our awareness and become more balanced.

How do you think yoga can help heal the body during a time of great shock and grief?

Yoga allows us to just be who we are, to feel what we are feeling. Grief and shock are normal responses to trauma and, while we may not be able to change our situation, yoga gives us the tools to adapt, adjust and accommodate to our new reality. We are invited to accept ourselves, just as we are, even if we don't recognise ourselves anymore. Through yoga practices, we can begin to sense some space around the feelings of despair, seeing that we are more than a grieving person.

We experience the possibility of holding opposing thoughts or emotions, such as joy and sorrow, at the same time.

Yoga is self-care practice, underpinned with compassion. When the body feels tight with shock and sorrow, yoga postures can raise our spirits and shift our energy, helping create a healthy, strong, flexible and vibrant body. Yogic breathing practices can have an immediate and positive effect on the nervous system, reducing stress hormones and promoting calm.

Yoga is also about relationships, inviting a deeper and more fulfilling connection to ourselves, our loved ones and those we have lost. If we refuse to deal with grief, we risk hardening ourselves to our own feelings and to those we love. As we use yoga to open our hearts and feel the goodness within us, we start to trust that we can become stronger.

How soon would you say someone could or should get into or back to practising yoga after the loss of a child?

Return to or begin yoga when you are ready. Your experience and response to loss and grief is unique to you. Be compassionate with yourself, trust yourself and give yourself permission to heal in whatever way feels natural. When you are overcome, and sleep is difficult, a gentle practice of restorative yoga postures can help to provide comfort, allowing any feelings, thoughts and emotions to naturally arise. A guided relaxation can provide respite from an agitated mind and a doorway to deep rest. Breathing practices encourage an emotional release, exhaling fear and sadness, breathing in life. There is real benefit in short practice whenever you need it – a few minutes of conscious breathing, meditation or mindful movement can help us to move from a place of inertia. Take one day at a time, one breath at a time.

Do you think that, in these circumstances, yoga is best practised at home or in a group/class?

Trust your intuitive wisdom. It's good to be supported by an experienced and qualified teacher, so find the person you resonate with and can trust. While virtual teachers online and in books can inspire and be a good way to begin, a personal teacher will help to mirror your inherent goodness and give you specific tools to help you on your healing journey. Your teacher should be compassionate and empower you to hear and trust your own inner teacher. When you can't face a group class, a home practice is wonderful as time for you to reconnect to the goodness within.

A group yoga class will often uplift us in ways we didn't think possible. Your yoga class should feel safe and welcoming, where space is held for everyone to explore their own individual needs and benefit from positive group energy. Group classes provide a community of like-minded people, and we come to see that everyone is faced with life challenges and struggles. Connect with others to share, laugh, experience joy and find support.

If you could offer one piece of advice to someone who has recently gone through the loss of a baby and is looking to start yoga, what would it be?

You are not alone, and you don't need to navigate this difficult time on your own. Yoga can help you to adjust and heal postnatally. In the early postnatal period, the body may be soft and weak, and in those first weeks yoga can help to provide an effective route to physical recovery. The emphasis should be on healing from the inside out, with breathing and gentle postures. As strength and stability returns, a more active practice can be included. Find a teacher you trust.

What, in your opinion, sets yoga apart from other kinds of well-being exercise and practices?

The tools of yoga are rich and diverse, and may include a good amount of exercise for the body, but fundamentally it's a healing practice intended to liberate us from the restrictions of our limited thinking, realigning mind, body and spirit. We learn that our thoughts create feelings, and our bodies experience, hold and express these feelings. As we become more aware of the mind–body connection, the better we can manage our thoughts and feelings. Rather than struggling with our reality, we can integrate our experiences of life so that we become fuller, not emptier.

Louise Rogers
www.louiserogersyoga.co.uk

REFLEXOLOGY

After getting back to yoga, I gained the confidence to start trying a few more things to help aid my recovery. It was about four months after Teddy had died and we were just starting to get some kind of rhythm back into our lives. Still being off work on maternity leave meant I had more time to explore my interests and think about trying things that would make me feel good about myself again. The first thing on the list was reflexology (a treatment massage that includes the feet and ankles). I knew a fair amount about it, having worked in spas that offered it and having friends who were trained in it. I'd been a 'case study' client for one of those friends when she was learning, many years ago, but I hadn't ever had a treatment just for my own benefit. That was about to change.

Balancing my hormones after Teddy was born had felt like a full-time job in itself. My cycles were totally out of whack and I felt like I didn't really know my body anymore. After having spoken to so many of my friends after my experience I now know this is entirely normal. Add some grief and shock into that mix and you've got yourself a cocktail for an emotional and hormonal disaster! I decided to try reflexology to help with all of the above.

Luckily, I found a wonderful practitioner at a clinic in my home town, so I was able to see her weekly. After just two treatments my cycles were back to a timely 28 days – you could set your watch by them! As someone who had suffered with lengthy cycles, missed periods and polycystic ovaries, this was the first time in a decade I felt 'normal'. In my eyes, this was nothing short of a miracle! Needless to say, I have continued with regular reflexology and it continues to help my recovery after losing Teddy. (I should also probably say that it is just so damn relaxing that you just fall asleep each time. It's win-win.)

I started to become one of those annoying people who recommended it to everyone I know, to help them with one thing or another in their life. I have a tendency to do that with things; it's like I think I have uncovered some huge secret that we should all know about and I have to tell the world about it, I just cannot help myself. Reflexology was no different to yoga in that respect, as it was helping me feel more confident when I spoke about Teddy, it was balancing my hormones, and I was sure that I was beginning to feel so much stronger again, after just a few months of treatments. There are so many alternative therapies out there, but in my humble opinion, this one really is worth trying if you are looking for something to help post-loss. I have asked my lovely friend and practitioner Angie to write a few words on exactly why.

What is reflexology and how would you describe its power to someone who didn't know about it?

Reflexology divides the body into ten zones, running horizontally from head to toes, and there are five zones on each side. A miniature map of all the zones and the individual organs found in them can be accessed via the feet, hands and ears. The power of reflexology comes from the fact that imbalances anywhere in the body can be detected and treated simply by touching and massaging the feet, hands or ears.

Reflexologists working in these areas use several mechanisms to bring about improvements in physical, mental and emotional well-being. These might include: unblocking of energy fields, the removal of toxins, the breakdown of crystalline deposits in the lymphatic system, the release of endorphins, alteration of electromagnetic fields and the increase of blood flow to internal organs.

How do you think reflexology can help heal the body during a time of great shock and grief?

Each person will react to and deal with great shock and grief in their own unique way. The list of health issues which may be experienced by someone experiencing this kind of trauma is almost endless and can vary from mild to quite serious conditions. Increased muscle tension, lack of sleep, loss of appetite and of course depression are some of the more common symptoms of a sudden increase in stress. Reflexology is mainly used to release tension and stress in the body. Research has shown it can increase serotonin levels in the brain, which are responsible for enhancing mood. Releasing stored toxins and increasing blood flow can also bring a greater sense of well-being, diminishing pain and improving sleep.

How soon would you say someone could or should have treatments after the loss of a child?

Self-care is a priority at all times, not just in a crisis. Taking time to nurture yourself during times of stress is especially important. There is no specific time constraint or rule that I could make, other than to seek help whenever you feel ready and it feels right for you.

Whether to seek treatment at home or in a clinic depends on the prevailing circumstances. If the client's trauma is such that they find it difficult or too stressful to leave their home, then the only option is a home treatment. Professional therapists of any type will be aware that effective treatments rely to a very large extent on the environment in which the treatment is conducted. Above all, clients must feel safe and relaxed, and the treatment area must be comfortable, clean and quiet. Most clinics are set up with all of this in mind. Some of these important factors can be difficult to control in the home, with other family members, pets and local noise conditions being a consideration. For this reason, it is usually better to see your therapist where they normally practise.

What, in your opinion, sets reflexology apart from other kinds of well-being practices and treatments?

As far as I am aware, reflexology is the only therapy that works with reflex zones in the body. These zones are different from the Chinese system of energy meridians and are not the same as the myofascial meridians used in some forms of manual therapy. The earliest records of some kind of foot and hand massage date back to wall paintings found in Egypt c. 2330 BC. An early form of reflexology (zone therapy) was introduced to the United States in 1913 by Dr William Fitzgerald, an ear, nose and throat specialist. The modern practice of reflexology is primarily influenced by the work of Eunice Ingham, a nurse and physiotherapist whose 1938 text *Stories the Feet Can Tell* contained detailed maps of the 'reflex' areas of the sole of the foot, corresponding to the rest of the body, including internal organs.

If you could offer one piece of advice to someone who has recently gone through the loss of a baby and is looking to reflexology, what would it be?

Reflexology is a totally non-invasive form of therapy, and so is safe even for those who may have recently been injured or undergone surgery. My advice for someone who would like to try reflexology is first to find a practitioner who you trust and feel comfortable sharing your personal issues and concerns with. Someone who can really listen and empathise with your experience, rather than a therapist who follows their own agenda or a set routine regardless of your individual needs – this is essential. If your therapist can help you feel safe, more relaxed, listened to, balanced and in less pain physically and/or emotionally, then you are on the right path.

Angie Ix Chel, MFHT
www.ixcheluk.co.uk

ACUPUNCTURE

The discovery I made last is probably the one that has had most impact on my general health and well-being since Teddy died; which is strange, because it's the one thing that the old me probably wouldn't have entertained trying. I don't have a phobia of needles, but like most of us I tend to try and avoid them when I can! I am, of course, talking about acupuncture. I think we all have a vision of what that means or what it entails, and mine was one of pain and torture, but I have no idea why this was. I also thought that acupuncture was something you had if you were in pain or had a cold you wanted gone, I didn't realise the huge help it could be for emotional and physical healing.

I actually first went to try it about six months after Teddy died for a pain in my shoulder and neck. I had slept awkwardly and the pain just wouldn't shift – it was making me feel sick and like I had a weight around my neck. What I didn't realise was that this discomfort was somewhat exaggerated by the emotional tension I was holding in my body.

After my first treatment I felt as though a physical weight had been lifted from me; I felt lighter. I tried to explain it to my husband, but I couldn't quite articulate how much better it had made me feel in myself. Just stronger somehow.

I began to go every week, and it became an even bigger help to me when we lost our second baby. I had been pregnant again when I started having acupuncture, our longed-for rainbow baby, but it wasn't meant to be. I called my acupuncturist and told her what had happened and she asked me to come in and see her for treatment as soon as I was able. I made an appointment to see her later that week, and that was over a year ago. As I write this now, I feel so fortunate to be able to say that my mind frame couldn't be more different from how I felt then.

No, I'm not pregnant again, but I hate to think how much slower my recovery would have been if I hadn't sought help outside of western medicine when I did. I am a true believer that we must do as much to help ourselves in these situations as we can; whether that is diet, lifestyle, choosing to take time out or focusing on self-care methods. I don't think that medicine or hospital treatment alone can 'fix' us, whatever is wrong. I think that true recovery is very much affected by a range of things, and many of those are things we can choose to do to help ourselves. For me, acupuncture enabled me to manage my emotions, to feel as though my head was lifted above that fog. Sometimes it made me cry, I mean really cry, and that was good, because I needed to. Sometimes I came out feeling as though all of my complicated thoughts had been neatly filed away in my head and were in some kind of order, so that I could go about my day again without them weighing me down. It made me feel free from the grief and worry that had shackled my existence for so many months. I felt strong and able to face each day; and so I continued, and still do.

I don't think that Gretchen will ever really understand or appreciate all that she has done to help me in the wake of Teddy's death – she is far too humble and kind – but here you can read in her own words why she believes acupuncture is so beneficial to someone who has been through trauma and loss.

What is acupuncture and how would you describe its power to someone who didn't know about it?

Acupuncture is a tried and tested system of complementary medicine. Chinese and other eastern cultures have been using acupuncture for over 2,000 years to promote and maintain good health, and restore the natural balance of the body.

According to traditional Chinese philosophy, our physical and emotional well-being is dependent on the balanced flow of energy. When the flow of 'qi' (energy) becomes injured, shocked or unbalanced, it can lead to ill health. By the insertion of fine needles into specific points along the channels of energy or meridians, acupuncture can stimulate the body's own healing response by removing blockages and helping to restore its natural balance.

Treating long-standing conditions, or where conventional treatments have not helped, more people are turning to acupuncture as a safe, natural form of medicine. There is significantly more conventional medical research being done to discover how acupuncture works as people are becoming more curious as to the mechanics of the process.

How do you think acupuncture can help heal the body during a time of great shock and grief?

Treatment would be recommended to subdue the emotional shock of loss but, in many instances, physiological stress can be lessened by promoting flow of oxygen and energy to various parts of the body. Treating the heart and spirit is an integral part of acupuncture, so we would not treat the body, mind and spirit separately.

How soon would you say someone could or should have treatments after the loss of a child?

During this very difficult time, people react differently to shock and stress. I would recommend immediate treatment. In stroke patients, it has been shown that recovery and rehabilitation is much improved by immediate acupuncture treatment. In saying that, not everyone is ready to start treatment right away. Shock and emotional trauma can be a very debilitating situation and patients may require time to adjust to the reality of the situation before they are able to seek help.

Why do you think acupuncture is beneficial to a mother's body after the loss of a pregnancy or the stillbirth or neonatal death of her child?

Firstly, acupuncture can assist with blood loss and the physical exhaustion of labour. By treating the kidneys, the blood and the person as a whole, treatment will assist the body's coping mechanism. A weakened body cannot support a shocked and grieving mind or heart, and a weakened emotional state cannot assist a weakened physical state. Acupuncture will assist in regaining homeostasis.

Do you think that, in these circumstances, treatments at home or at a clinic/practice environment are best?

This is a difficult question to answer but, having treated in both environments, I may suggest that a clinic visit is attempted rather than staying at home. Patients may only feel safe at home during this time, but getting patients 'out of the house', where all their grief will be surrounding them, can only be a good thing in my opinion. Patients can feel isolated and even scared to face the world, but this will ease with time.

What, in your opinion, sets acupuncture apart from other kinds of alternative medicines and treatments?

Acupuncture treats the 'whole' as many other therapies do, but I think the one thing that sets it apart from others is the fact that we can tap into the physiological as well as the spiritual side of the person. By 'spiritual', I mean we can treat the patient's spirit and heart directly. This is a key factor in successful treatment of trauma.

If you could offer one piece of advice to someone who has recently gone through the loss of a baby and is looking to start acupuncture, what would it be?

You may think you are ready to try again immediately, but until your body, mind and spirit are strong and in alignment, let time and nature help you and your body come to terms with the loss. I don't believe people ever get over the loss of a child, but they can process the feelings associated with such a trauma.

Patients describe that a 'space' is always there. In my opinion, this is a healthy and natural observation. A soul has visited their lives, although they have now moved on, and acceptance and healing seems to occur when this is acknowledged. Give your body and spirit time to adjust to the loss. Psychic shock will take its own time to heal but, with treatment, this process can be aided. Acupuncture has proven itself to many patients in giving them the ability to allow the healing process to occur in situations of extreme loss, and that they can go on to have successful pregnancies.

Gretchen Smit BSc (Hons) LicAc
www.gretchensmit.com

There have also been a few other things I have done and have used in order to aid a positive mind-set. Lots of people write to me and ask, 'How do you stay so happy?' I won't lie, I'm not grinning manically every day of my life, but I don't feel that huge depth of sadness like I once did; and I think I have many of these things to thank for that.

SAYING NO

There have been so many other little adaptations I have made in my life in a bid to 'feel better'. Some are the simple ones like just saying 'no' when you feel overloaded, as I touched on in Chapter 16. Although I say that as if it is a simple thing to do, I honestly don't think that many of us even realise (especially when we are knee-deep in grief) that that *is* totally acceptable. I know we all feel guilt, but sometimes we just have to be kind to ourselves and accept that not trying to please everyone all of the time will help our road to recovery.

AFFIRMATION CARDS

A few months after Teddy died, I bought myself some 'Yes Mum' affirmation cards on the recommendation of a friend. They were 'Strength' cards, that help to affirm those feelings of strenth during loss or testing times. I got in the habit of always carrying one with me, in my pocket or my bag, and just looking at it when I needed strength during loss or testing times to. It was a simple little tactic, and some might think it sounds completely mad, but in those moments that I just needed that little boost it was like having someone there who was telling me it was going to be OK. I think that when you are suffering with grief-related anxieties, it really helps to have tools like that, especially if you are on a crowded train or in a busy place. It's that little nod of reassurance; at least that is how it felt for me.

POSITIVITY JOURNAL

Not long after I started writing my blog, a wonderful woman called Kelly contacted me through Instagram, who I instantly warmed to. She told me her story, that her darling mum was battling with Huntington's disease, and that she had started a business off of the back of that journey. She had developed a positivity journal – something to fill in at the end of each day to help you to appreciate the little things in life, to help with your general wellness and mental well-being. Kelly asked if she could send me one as a gift.

I started filling it in the day it arrived. It meant filling in things like what had felt good that day, what had I done for myself, as well as other details like water intake and hours of sleep. It felt so empowering to focus on the little victories, to reflect on all that was great about life, even on the more challenging days. It was a place to write in all of my achievements (however small) and a place to write goals. It meant I could write down affirmations for the month ahead, or thoughts and feelings I was aiming to leave behind. For me, it was the perfect way to help my heart recover – seeing all of these things in one place, on the page in front of me.

I completed 365 days of that journal. A complete snapshot of my year – probably one of the most difficult I have faced, but yet I am still here. Looking at that journal I can see how far I have come and how much better I feel in myself. It reminds me of what it felt like to have lost two babies so close together and why my body, and mind, needed that extra time to heal and recover from such trauma. I feel enormously proud of how far I have come during that year, and so very excited for the next 365 days that lay ahead of me.

★

There is no rulebook; there is no right or wrong answer here, so stop searching for it. We are all different, we all react to situations differently, and losing a child is no different. So, write, sing, run, raise money, organise a bloody bake sale (I have yet to try that one, but I have donated cakes to the NICU once, so I am claiming that as involvement); do what channels you in the wake of your disaster. Why? Because it just makes everything feel so much better and, when you've been at your lowest ebb, sometimes even the tiniest crack of light can feel like a whole day of sunshine.

Chapter 18

It's Not Just Me

IT'S NOT JUST ME, I KNOW THAT. THE RIPPLES OF EMOTION CAUSED BY TEDDY'S SWIFT ENTRANCE AND EXIT FROM THIS WORLD GO FURTHER THAN I WILL PROBABLY EVER BE ABLE TO UNDERSTAND. Losing a child shocks an entire family, and their friends, beyond comprehension. I am only too aware that much of the writing found online about child loss is written by the child's mother. That it is the mother from whom we expect to be able to learn the full story of what it feels like, what it *is* like, when a baby dies. I have always said, when anyone has complimented anything I have written about Teddy, that it's not about me, I am simply telling *his* story. I want him to be celebrated in the world and talked about, and luckily for me, so do our family and friends. With that in mind, allow me to let them share their side of Teddy's story with you all.

Nico
Teddy's daddy

When people used to ask me what we were having during Elle's pregnancy, my answer was always the same: an Olympic gold medallist. I'd envisage being the dad on the sidelines or shipping them to various activities, just as my parents did with me.

I've been fortunate enough in life to only visit hospitals due to my own stupidity – from bulging discs in my back, rupturing shoulder ligaments, to severely dehydrating during a marathon, it's always been my fault. Elle's pregnancy went without a hitch and I never for once thought that anything bad could ever go wrong. Why would it? We are (or were?) both young, healthy and have a healthy family history – I obviously checked as part of my thorough breeding programme prior to popping the question to her...!

When the consultant sat us down after one of the nurses ran off with Teddy, he told us Teddy was a really sick boy. At that stage my barometer for 'sick' meant that he'd have to be looked after for a couple of days before coming home, but not at any point did I think it would be worse than that. When we were transferred to the neonatal intensive care unit, things started to sink in, slowly but surely – the receptionist who knew our names before we introduced ourselves, the looks on the nurse's face when they saw you, the head tilts. They were all subliminally telling me things were far worse than I expected. Of course, all day and every day we sat next to Teddy, watching the brain monitors, hoping to see a flicker of movement. Sometimes my brain would trick me into seeing something and Elle would say she didn't see it; other times Elle was the one telling me she had seen something.

The hardest thing in those three days was seeing the pain Elle was going through. Twenty-one hours of labour takes its toll on every woman, but this was another stage of endurance no one had planned on. Going through labour, having no sleep, and then having the stress of rushing to an intensive care unit was a huge strain on her body and mind. It's when people are under pressure that you find out what their characters are really like, and I couldn't have been more bursting with pride as I watched her looking over Teddy. I could see her giving him every ounce of the little energy she had left, and then some. It was quite incredible to see what she was capable of under such straining circumstances.

Saying goodbye to Teddy and the days after will remain etched in my mind. He was surrounded by love as he took his last breaths, and isn't that what we all want? I remember leaving the hospital and my father and brother-in-law ran ahead and moved the baby seat into the boot of the car so we wouldn't have to look at it, another reminder on the journey home.

I soon learned, though, that there was no escaping losing Teddy. We'd had nine months to prepare. A house full of stuff, a tight-knit street, friends and work colleagues to tell. Elle just couldn't get the words out so I tried to tell as many people as possible and let them spread the word.

Then there was the recovery. How do you recover? Well, it turns out there isn't a simple recipe to follow. But let's be clear – if there was, I'd still struggle, as it takes me two hours to cook a 30-minute meal recipe from any well-known cook. So I used my father's expression, 'If you've got to eat an elephant, do it in small pieces.'

I started to hate sitting down doing nothing. It wasn't getting me or Elle anywhere, and the days would go so slowly. I had in my mind that the days needed to pass so that the pain would go away, so I began to wish time away. I suddenly realised that it wasn't time that was the problem, though, it was my mind. I took up woodwork to keep busy in the house, and it was perfect. Something that kept my mind and hands busy. There's something intensely therapeutic about taking raw untouched material and putting your sweat into it (and definitively blood, on a few occasions) to create something to share. The table that sits in our dining room, for example. There are times when we sit around it with friends and family and I drift away, Teddy being ever present in my mind. It remains my favourite thing in the house.

Going back to work was actually something I began to look forward to. I remember sitting on the train on the first day, though, and it felt like an outer-body experience. The train gang that I sit near (but don't partake of their daily banter – way too early in the day for that) were cracking the same jokes they had been three weeks ago, as if nothing had changed. All I could think was, *How can they carry on like this? Don't they realise that the whole world came to a standstill three weeks ago?* It dawned on me straight away that the whole world didn't stop like it did for us.

I nervously walked into work and the first thing my boss said was, 'Your haircut makes you look like an idiot.' It was that level of normality that was just what I needed. That being said, I immediately felt guilty for leaving Elle at home. She was really struggling. Deep down I knew that this would be the end of her current job, and that I may have to take the strain financially to allow her to heal emotionally for a while. It was my way of helping the family. We still had an extra mouth to feed after all, even though he was just 30cm tall (Boris). Work was fantastic in letting me take the odd day to work from home – they couldn't have handled the situation better, and they were quite incredible. I was very fortunate.

To say people were treading on eggshells was an understatement, so I sent an email to everyone asking them to treat me like they would have if Teddy had come home. I wasn't afraid to talk about him, and I'd rather everyone knew. There were the odd howlers – about four weeks later someone came up to me and shook my hand congratulating me on having a baby in front of a few colleagues. He hadn't got the email, so I had to tell him. It's actually those people who I felt sorry for, and 'Do you have any children?' is still the hardest question I get asked. I meet a lot of casual acquaintances through work and I make the decision that if I'm ever going to see them again I say yes, and if I'm not I say no. It's just not worth ruining their light-hearted, polite conversation.

About a year after Teddy died, I was at a dinner and someone asked me, 'What do you do for fun?' It suddenly dawned on me that, for the twelve months, we had just been in survival mode. Fun wasn't really something I'd bothered with or thought about. Every weekend had been about spending time together, healing in our own little world, going on the odd outing – but generally, doing 'things' wasn't on the list. This has slowly changed. Activities like going for dinner, or coffee, going out to the cinema or some drinks with friends – all of the little things we had shied away from, finally we are now starting to do.

Except, I do them now with a much deeper appreciation. I've always been quite a calm guy (or so I've been told) but this experience has mellowed me out completely. Very few things stress me since we lost Teddy, because of those three days in the NICU with him. (I do still rage at my commute on the trains every now and then, but that's for another time.)

I'm just grateful to have all those that I love around me and in good health, and I feel like a richer person for having had Teddy in our lives to bring me that perspective. I've learned that the start of a life and the end of a life can, and should, bring us to a standstill – everything else is just details.

Carol
Teddy's grandma and my darling mummy

When people ask me how many grandchildren I have, I tell them that I have four. Teddy was the third to be born. He came into the world on Monday, 16th May 2016, but could only stay with us for three days. I wish I could have been there to see him when he was first born, but it was late evening by the time he finally made his appearance, so too late for hospital visiting.

When Eleanor called me before eight o'clock the following morning, I knew straight away that something was not right by the tone of her voice. I asked her how everyone was and she replied, 'Not good, Mummy.' She explained to me what had happened during the night, that Teddy had been resuscitated after many minutes and that they were being transferred to another hospital where there were specialist facilities to treat him. As soon as we found out which hospital they were going to, Ian, my husband, and I set out to drive to Chertsey to visit our new grandson for the first time.

I think we both spent the journey trying to reassure one another that modern medicine could indeed work wonders these days in the face of seemingly impossible odds, and that surely Teddy was going to be treated for whatever was wrong and he would be fine. Despite our forced optimism, I don't think we were prepared for the sight of such a beautiful little man covered in wires and tubes, lying in his plastic 'tank'. He had a fuzz of fluffy hair and such a cherubic face, it seemed impossible that he wouldn't wake up any second and be just fine.

The next time we went to visit, on Thursday, 19th May, would turn out to be the last time we saw that lovely face. The doctors treating Teddy said that they wanted to sit down with Eleanor and Nico to speak to them about his situation. Eleanor asked if Ian and I could be included in the meeting too. I can't really remember the exact words that the doctors used. Teddy was, it seemed, not able to stay with us, as his body simply was not able to function. His metabolism would not 'fire up' and do the necessary job to make him viable without his life support. His condition was deteriorating fast. It seemed strange that they had done so many tests and yet still had no specific reason why this was the case.

The thing that stands out in my mind above all else about the moments following the explanation is that the only one who managed to ask questions about his condition was Eleanor. The rest of us sat crying and mute, while my brave daughter, fighting for her son to the last second, asked whether Teddy would be suffering any pain because of his condition.

Within that half an hour meeting, Nico and Eleanor had given their consent to Teddy's ventilator to be switched off, but they asked whether they could hold him and read to him in the privacy of the parents' room with the rest of his family around. Nico's parents and his sister and brother-in-law returned that afternoon to be with Teddy, too. Watching him leave us was one of the hardest things I have ever had to do, but watching my daughter's heart break as she held her son was just as hard. I wanted so much to be able to help her; to make things right again. When our children are young we can help them to cope with just about anything. A hug or a treat if they fall over, a chat and a takeaway pizza when they are teenagers with boyfriend or girlfriend problems. This time, there was nothing I could say or do to make it all go away. I felt powerless and grief-stricken all at once.

In the days that followed, Ian and I stayed with Nico and Elle to make sure that they ate properly and had someone there to talk to or cry on. Much talking and crying went on in the days following Teddy's death. Looking back, I think it helped us all. It didn't make anything better, but it certainly helped.

It was difficult to leave Nico and Eleanor alone with an empty nursery, but we had to go back to Dorset after a few days. We spoke every day on FaceTime, sharing our thoughts about anything and everything to do with Teddy. They had to deal with the practical administrative aspects of birth and death, which seemed so unbearably unjust when we had all been waiting for a new baby to join the family. Certificates had to be issued and a post-mortem had to be done too. It was all a million miles away from what we expected to be doing in the weeks following Teddy's birth.

About six weeks later we had a funeral for our darling Teddy. It was completely unlike any funeral I had been to. Those had been for much older family members who had lived a whole life. Teddy was not given the chance to be all that we imagined and dreamed of.

In the months that followed, I was just there as much as possible whenever Eleanor needed me to be. We cried and laughed. We tried our hands at new crafts:

lampshade making, upholstery, wreath-making, you name it! We shopped, we lunched, we sewed, we gardened, then we cried some more. I suppose you could say we were keeping busy to distract ourselves, which is probably true, but it helped us both and brought us closer than ever.

As the time has passed and Teddy's Legacy has become a focus of Eleanor's life, I have been astounded all over again at how amazing the young woman is that I am proud to call my daughter. She has had good days and bad days, but I think (and hope) that the good now outweigh the bad. Teddy is always in our hearts and we talk about him often, because he has changed us all. The ripples have spread throughout our family and we have all been changed since he was born. Yes, I have four grandchildren. There will be more I'm sure, but Teddy will *always* be the third.

Amanda

Not just one of my closest friends, but one of my all-time favourite humans. Also, one of the few people who was able to make me laugh out loud in the weeks that followed losing Teddy. Basically, she's an all-round hero and my favourite 'wee Scot'.

When I found out the news that Teddy had passed away, just like everyone else I was so shocked and numb. Truthfully, it just didn't feel real – *this surely wasn't happening*, was all I could think. You read about these tragedies and, although they make you sad, your reaction and sadness are very temporary when you hear of it happening to people you do not know. You never think it could ever possibly happen to someone you know, and even more so someone you love and care for dearly. All you think is, *No way, this is not real, it isn't true!* I genuinely did not take it in.

I remember immediately thinking of Elle and feeling impossibly paralysed, helpless to a friend that deserved everything in the world. Why was this happening and why to her? Over the coming days and weeks after Teddy's death, truthfully, I felt so helpless – I knew I couldn't do anything to soften or even pause her pain. I felt uncomfortable about contacting her and reaching out – that's the reality and truth from my side. You want *so* much to have something, whether it is words or anything else, that could comfort her, but I felt speechless and useless. I don't have children myself, so this made me feel all the more useless.

The few days after Teddy died we exchanged a few texts and I remember vividly the feeling of my heart just sinking for her. I couldn't and didn't even attempt to fathom her pain – it wasn't for me to try or attempt. I could only hope that I could be of comfort at some point. I deliberately didn't overdo it in contacting her. I knew that Nico and close family would be there every moment, and I was conscious to hold back in those first few weeks. I think as a very close friend and knowing Elle well, that this minimal contact approach was actually the best way. Elle would have had endless texts, calls, flowers, all a reminder of what happened. I didn't want to do that too. It might sound odd, but it did feel like the right thing to do. Not to take from anyone's love and thoughts for her, but I knew she would have had more messages to absorb and take in from everyone, and the sheer volume of outpouring from others would've been overwhelming. I was conscious to tell her I was thinking of her – I was, constantly – but didn't want to force contact or the opportunity to meet up. I knew it would be a few weeks before she would be able to see me, so I gave her the space and time, a few texts in-between, and eventually we arranged to meet at her house.

This had never happened to anyone I knew, so I didn't ask anyone what I should say or do. I looked online and I took a few pieces of advice on board, but I was so nervous to see her. I remember even shaking on the train down to hers. What to say, would we still joke like we used to? That's all Elle and I ever do – laugh and joke. I almost felt frightened that I was about to encounter a complete stranger, someone a shadow of their former self, unrecognisable.

I always remember Elle opening her front door that day and she gave me the hugest hug. In that moment, although you could see and feel her pain, it was still Elle. Even now, thinking of that day makes me feel really emotional. I am not overtly emotional and certainly our friendship had never really been one where we had cried or been sad really at any point. We were jokers – when we had worked together I am sure the laughter got on most of our colleague's nerves. She was still the same old Elle cracking jokes, making me laugh, asking about me and my life. She had been through simply the worst thing anyone could ever go through and here she was asking about how things were with me. Perhaps it was her way of escaping for that moment, but I was more than happy to be that escape for her.

I couldn't ever imagine the constant sadness that not only she felt, but which emanated from others when they met with her. That must've been exhausting –

it probably still is – so that day it was about talking about what she was comfortable with. When we started to chat about Teddy, although watching her get upset was uncomfortable and not nice to watch, it was so important to talk about him. She had sent me a few pictures the day he was born and when she spoke of him I remember just creating this wee place in my heart for him. I won't lie, that day wasn't easy, but being a friend and giving your support – whether that's by having a joke or a laugh about something silly, or talking about Teddy – was paramount. I left Elle's that day feeling so glad I got to see her and hoped I had given her some respite.

After that, and obviously still now, Elle and I meet up frequently. Often, I will go down and visit her and Nico (and Boris of course ☺) and we laugh and joke as we always did before. Her sense of humour is well intact, and she is simply one of the funniest and smartest people I have the pleasure of knowing. We chat about Teddy and her experience too, and she of course gets upset, but now I just understand that that's part of talking about him – I always wish to hear about him.

He wasn't with us for very long, but what an impact that little boy has made. I am so proud of the work she has done to build awareness around child loss, and even more proud of her endless strength, humour and kindness. Elle is one special lady, and I am super grateful and blessed to have her as a friend.

Zoe

Teddy's aunty and Nico's big sister. One of the first people to be by our sides at the NICU, and one of the few people who got to meet Teddy, hold him and talk to him. I don't have a sister, but I feel very lucky now to feel like I have found one.

As Nico and I walked into the intensive care unit, my heart was pounding in my chest. I knew Teddy was very sick but I had no idea what to expect. Yet, despite all the wires and machines keeping him alive, he was gorgeous. I reached into the incubator and stroked his soft, downy blond hair and his little bare arms. He had the softest skin I had ever touched. He was perfect and I told Nico that.

Over the next few hours, I watched as doctors and nurses buzzed around him. I found myself desperately scanning their faces for signs that Teddy was going to be OK, but they gave nothing away. Like all new parents, Nico and Elle looked shell-shocked. It had been a normal pregnancy and a normal birth and yet, now, instead of having those first precious few hours getting to know their son, they weren't even allowed to hold him. They spent hours by his side, and when they had meetings with the doctors, we all took it in turns to sit with him.

I kept telling myself that Teddy was going to be fine, that this would be nothing more than a nasty scare. I was convinced that if we talked to Teddy, sang to him, touched him, we could make him come back to us. As I sat with my nephew, I made so many promises to him. I told him that he had the best parents in the world and that if he could just get better we were going to have such fun. I told him that his mummy was besotted with him and was going to smother him with kisses and cuddles, that his daddy would teach him how to drop-kick and to speak French, that he and his cousins would spend hours racing around in the garden with Boris. 'Please come back to us, Teddy,' I begged, over and over.

All of Nico and Elle's friends lit candles for Teddy and we asked our friends to as well. Somehow it seemed important that people knew that a little boy called Teddy was fighting for his life. So many people did it, all willing him to pull through.

On the second evening in the NICU, Elle and I sat on either side of Teddy's incubator. His tiny body kept on convulsing with seizures and it was agony to watch. I didn't want him to be in pain or to hurt himself, and I didn't want Nico and Elle to have to see him like this. Elle and I gently placed our hands on his arms and legs and tried to keep him safe. She stroked him over and over, begging her little boy to come back to her. Nico said Teddy looked like a little chick, trying to fly, and I was so scared that was what he was doing – I was so scared he was flying away from us.

By the third day, it became obvious that there were few positives left to cling to. Teddy was so tiny and his poor body had already been through so much. Nico and Elle were relentlessly positive but I felt sick to my stomach that he wasn't going to make it.

I needed some fresh air and went and sat by a pond and listened to the birds singing. As children and families ran around in the beautiful spring sunshine, I prayed for Teddy like I had never prayed before. I wondered if I hadn't been trying hard enough and I just needed to try harder. It was while I was sitting there that I got the phone call to say that there was nothing more they could do; they were going to let Teddy go. I don't even remember what I said to Nico and Elle, but the sadness in their eyes will haunt me forever. I was Nico's big sister and I had looked out for him from day one, and yet I couldn't protect him from any of this pain.

Now the worst was happening, Nico and Elle's focus was purely on their little boy. I might have been tempted to shut the world out and be alone with my son, but they wanted him to be surrounded by family so he would feel how loved he was. They even asked if any of us would like to hold him. I hesitated for a second. I knew how painful it would be and yet I couldn't say no. My mum and Elle's mum both wanted to have a cuddle as well but neither my dad nor Elle's dad were able to; it was just too much for them.

First I watched my mum hold her new grandson. She looked so proud and so in love with Teddy, and also so heartbroken. Then it was my turn. Teddy's nurse gently lifted him into my arms, carefully arranging the wires so the machines could keep him breathing. I held him against my chest and he felt so soft and warm. As I kissed the top of Teddy's head and nestled him into me, I felt like my heart was shattering. It was a pain like nothing else I had ever experienced. Nico took a picture of me and Teddy – our one and only picture together.

We left Nico and Elle alone with Teddy after that. They held him, washed him and dressed him – all of the things that you take for granted as a parent, but it would be their first and final time. It felt like time slowed to a stop as we waited for the end. We were all crying, lost in our own worlds.

Teddy's nurse's 12-hour shift had finished, but she asked if she could stay and be with him at the end. I had never known kindness and humanity like it. She hand-pumped oxygen into Teddy's mouth until Nico and Elle were ready. Then she removed the oxygen, and they held their son on their laps and read *Guess How Much I Love You* to him.

It was a book I had read countless times to my daughter Daisy, but I knew that I would never be able to read it again. They took it in turns to read the words until Teddy stopped breathing. As I watched my nephew die, it was the most awful and the most humbling experience of my life.

Somehow, Nico and Elle tucked their little boy into his blankets and then the nurses took him away. I remember thinking that, if it were me, I wouldn't have had the strength to let him go. I still don't know how they did it.

My little brother was such a giant of a man. We'd

always been so close but now suddenly I had no idea how to comfort him or Elle. I couldn't bear the thought of them driving home with Teddy's car seat in the back, to an empty house and an empty Moses basket. Everything was torture for them, but when Elle's milk came in I felt like screaming at the universe for its unbearable cruelty. Wasn't it enough that she hadn't been able to take her baby home?

Eventually the day of Teddy's funeral arrived. As his coffin was brought into church it nearly destroyed every single one of us. It was so small it took just one man to carry it. Nothing about this was right. The natural order of life had been broken. My brother and his wife should never have been saying goodbye to their baby. Even now, I have no idea how I stood at the front and spoke about Teddy but I am so glad that I did. I spoke about all of the hopes and dreams we'd had for him, and I promised him that we would never, ever forget him.

In those first few weeks all we wanted was to make things better, to somehow take away some of Nico and Elle's pain, and that was the single hardest thing to come to terms with. Nothing could make it better. None of the stupid holidays we suggested, or seeing people, nothing worked – but of course it couldn't. You can't make things better after the death of a child. It was hideous being around my parents' pain too. They looked lost and helpless and I was so worried about them. For the first time in my life, I felt like our roles had reversed. Instead of celebrating a new grandchild, they were witnessing their son in unimaginable pain and they couldn't do anything to stop it.

We were all dealing with it differently. It felt like the women in both families needed to endlessly talk about Teddy, whereas the men hadn't a clue what to do other than throw themselves back into work and normal life, whatever that was now.

It was during this blur of sadness and grief that I discovered I was pregnant. It was a much longed-for baby, and yet the timing could not have been worse. I was petrified on so many levels – I'd recently had two miscarriages and I was terrified of having another one, but I was even more scared that I wouldn't. How could something positive come out of something so tragic, and how would I ever tell Nico and Elle?

In the end, they were amazing, as they always are. But my shame and the sickening guilt I felt didn't dissipate for the entire nine months. Nor did my fear. I'd watched my nephew die and now nothing would ever be the same again. Even as I gave birth, I never expected to take home a living baby. As my daughter, Amelie, was placed in my arms, I wept for her and I wept for Teddy. She was the first baby I'd held since Teddy and to me she felt like a gift from him. I made a promise to myself then that when she and Daisy grow up, they will know all about their little cousin, Teddy, and how special he was.

I have absolutely no doubt that Nico and Elle will be parents again and we will love their sons or daughters more than they can ever imagine. Yet no one can ever replace Teddy or the Teddy-shaped hole that has been left in our lives. He is missing from every family occasion. Whenever we are all together I am aware that a little blond boy should be laughing along with us, tearing around with his cousins and his sidekick Boris. At times I find family occasions and milestones like birthdays, Mother's Day and Father's Day torturous. I am painfully aware of Nico and Elle's feelings and my guilt at having two healthy children never goes away. I know we must unintentionally say and do the wrong things all the time because we aren't experts in this, we are all just stumbling our way through life after losing Teddy.

I have watched the way Nico and Elle have handled

themselves since Teddy's death in total awe. I am beyond proud of them. Thanks to their big hearts and the fundraising they have done in his name, so many people have been touched by Teddy, the little boy who was with us for such a short time yet has left such a huge impact. I am so proud to call myself Teddy's aunty.

If I could, I would take away every single ounce of Nico and Elle's heartache, and yet I can't wish away those three precious days with Teddy. The joy and love they felt at being his parents can never be taken away from them. Not a single day goes by when I don't think about him. The memory of him has been burned indelibly in me. I can still remember his smell and how soft his skin was. Now when I see the brightest star, a breath-taking sunset, a lone robin in the hedgerow or when I feel the sea breeze on my face, I think of Teddy. That little boy has changed our lives forever and we will never, ever forget him.

Chapter 19

Moving Forward, Not On

I SUPPOSE THAT THE MOST IMPORTANT QUESTION, FOR SOME PEOPLE, MIGHT BE: *HOW* DO WE MOVE ON FROM THIS? How on earth does anyone move on from this? As I have said previously, my desire in those early days of loss were very much to 'feel better', although I couldn't fathom how that might come about, but never have I had a desire to 'move on' from Teddy. Why would I? He is our son, our firstborn, and he will always be a huge part of our family. I know that it can also be used as a figure of speech and that people don't necessarily realise the impact of what they are implying when using a turn of phrase like that, but I can tell you that it can *really* hurt.

Quite recently I was subject to some vitriolic comments that every now and again rear their ugly heads through the pixels of social media. It doesn't happen very often, but when it does it usually ends in me overthinking the reasoning behind the remark. Perhaps I give the writer of such material more credit than they deserve? Either way, if I choose to write about Teddy and our journey since losing him, then other people are also free to form their own opinions on what I am doing – such is the world that we live in. The comment was, in my opinion, quite emotionally unintelligent. 'The more you talk about him the more you are opening up a wound and not allowing it to heal. Tragic things happen, accept and move on.' It was those last two words that rung in my ears: 'move on'. Surely this human, whoever they were, had never lost a child. Move on? Pretend it hadn't happened, that they hadn't existed?

They were telling me I shouldn't talk about Teddy; insinuating that I was dragging up the past and not allowing myself to heal. I thought long and hard on it, on where a remark like that could have stemmed from. I wanted to scream and shout at that person, to shake them and make them fully comprehend the hurtful nature of their words – but what would be the point in that? Would it change their mind or open their eyes to the reality of living after the loss of a child? Probably not. My initial reaction would have been peppered with fairly strong language, and I didn't want that to detract from me giving the response to that comment that I felt Teddy deserved me to give.

I fully accept and respect that we all grieve differently, but no matter how hard I focused on trying to understand their viewpoint, I simply could not. Firstly, this person had referred to Teddy as a 'wound'. Let's be really clear on this one: my son is *not* a wound, nor a scar I should be ashamed of. I will not be embarrassed to speak his name in fear that it might upset someone else, or not allow my heart to heal. In fact, the more I speak about him, the more freely that I am able to articulate my feelings surrounding his death, and so the more I begin to heal. I have seen a direct correlation between how much I am able to talk about Teddy and how much better I feel for doing so.

My son is not a dirty little secret who will not be spoken about in public, and I have learned that I am able to connect with so many other parents who have had similar experiences by talking about him. I wholeheartedly disagree with this person's view point that speaking about him is more damaging than it is cathartic, and I can only assume that this individual was brought up in a time when 'sweeping things under the carpet' and pretending that they hadn't happened was the 'done' thing. I can tell you that this *was* the case many years ago, and that it did a family member no good at all to harbour their experiences and feelings for over 65 years before being able to even whisper their child's name. So, no – I refuse to accept that not speaking about Teddy is the best course of action, and that is my prerogative, as his mother. Talking is *good*.

Now we come to the interesting part – the simple suggestion that we might just 'move on'. Well, random stranger on the internet, I can also tell you that just isn't a possibility for our family. You see, when something of such magnitude happens to you, whether it is the loss of a loved one, a tragic event or perhaps the suffering of a life-changing illness, it often shakes you to the very core of your being. It flips on its head what you believed to be true in the world and it magnifies the fragility of life and all that we often take for granted. It isn't just a loss, just an event you could pretend didn't happen – the very nature of its enormity changes you as a person forever, whether you are willing to accept that and identify those changes or not.

Something like losing a child changes the course

of your life, unrecognisably, forever. There is always someone missing, always, no matter how hard you try to pretend that isn't the case. Even if you don't say their name out loud, or you act as if it hasn't happened, it has. The more you bury it, the more it will always beg to be let to the surface, and the only person who will suffer is *you*, more so than you have already had to. I believe that by continuing to talk about Teddy I am letting the world know that I'm not scared of speaking about him, and that they are free to do so too. It's like giving everyone a hall-pass not to be terrified of the unspeakable, and just letting them, well, talk about it.

I often wonder what it might have been like if I were now two years on from losing Teddy and I had tried to just 'get on with it' and pretend he hadn't existed. Would I still spend the time I had, on my own, sobbing? Would I look at other people with children and feel envy and sadness? Would I constantly feel like I was denying myself the title of being a mother, even though I was one? Yes, I think the answer to all of the above is most likely, yes. I can't see how that could be considered 'moving on', because you're not really moving anywhere, are you? You're just pretending it hasn't bloody happened when it *has*. The thought of saying 'No' when I am asked if I have any children, without so much as a flinch; the idea of not having photos of him in our house or keepsakes with his name on. That vision, the one where we just erase him from our family tree in an effort to feel better, that is one that makes me feel very sad indeed. Sad for Teddy and sad for us that we would deny his existence for the benefit of the outside world feeling less 'awkward'.

I have come to realise that I don't actually want to 'move on'. The further away May 2016 becomes, the more and more Teddy's physical existence in this world is left in the past. All we physically have now is a box of his ashes, a few things we have in his memory box, and exactly 35 photos of him. (Let's face it, most mums take 35 photos a day on their phones now.) That's all we have, and the physical moments that Teddy was here with us are being left further behind. I take so much pride in all of those physical possessions we have that keep us connected to Teddy, but by talking about him we are keeping his energy alive, and allowing his memory and his legacy in this world to be part of our family life. He is not something I want to move on from, he is our son; and I most certainly will never 'move on' from being his mother.

I *do* believe that there are many things in life that we can move on from. Old relationships and friendships, jobs, interests or events that have taken place in our lives. I also think that it's pretty normal to do so, and I am not one of those people who keeps mementos of the tiniest occasion in life so that I can hang on to the memory. That suggestion that it would be a good idea, healthy even, to move on from the tragic death of a loved one, well, it quite simply baffled me – and I think it will do for a long time yet!

I am proud that Teddy is spoken about, proud that in speaking his name other people feel empowered to do the same, and proud that he will stay very much in this moment with us. I know it's not just me as I have since spoken to many parents who have lost and they all feel the same. I just hope that whoever made that remark wasn't someone who had experienced a loss and had been made to feel like that was the only way to deal with it by the people they had been surrounded by. I can only imagine that would be a truly sad and isolating place in which to exist.

I do also believe in moving forward. It is something I have written about and spoken about on so many occasions when addressing how we have coped with our new reality since Teddy's death. How do you move forward and start to make positive steps to living your life again, to actually enjoying things again, without that familiar pang of guilt washing over you and sucking the joy out of anything that once brought a smile to your face? I really wish I had a magic potion: 'Here, drink this, and you'll be able to enjoy yourself again.' (I think every grieving parent could do with one of these on the odd occasion.) As we all know, it's just not that straightforward, but I do passionately believe that there are simple steps you can take that allow you to nudge yourself in the right direction. For me, that has been looking after myself, taking time to enjoy things that I do love. I have never rushed back into feeling better or forced myself to do something if I thought that I wasn't physically or emotionally able.

Lots of parents who lose children feel that overwhelming desire to try for another baby. When you lose a baby the mix of emotions that rush through you are intense. Shock, grief, love, anger, shame; you name it, I probably felt it in those early weeks. The disbelief that what has happened is even real. Then eventually your subconscious catches up. For me, as that mist cleared, there was another emotion that took over, although I wouldn't liken it to any 'emotion' I had ever felt before. It was an overwhelming feeling, an *instinct*, that I *needed* to be pregnant again. My body knew that I wasn't holding a baby in my arms;

the hormones raging around inside me were telling my brain that something had gone horribly wrong and that I needed to do something about it. It wasn't a conscious decision, a discussion of 'we need to try again'; it was every inch of my being yearning for a baby to hold. Not to replace Teddy, not ever, but perhaps to help my broken heart and empty arms.

At moments, I felt so callous; why was I even considering having another baby? We hadn't even had our son's funeral at this point, and this thought, this instinct, kept shoving its way to the forefront of my mind. I couldn't quash it, no matter how hard I wanted it to disappear so that I could just grieve for Teddy in peace. It burned into me, every single moment.

I spoke to Nico and explained what I was thinking, how it was making me feel, how I needed to be a mother; not just to Teddy, but to another baby. He agreed that he thought we should think about trying again; and so, our journey of trying to conceive after loss began. I know that from speaking with my friends who have lost children that they too felt the same almost immediately after losing their children. It's that instinct to mother, to protect and to love. I don't for one second think that growing our family or having another baby will replace Teddy, but it would give me another little person to pour all of that love into, that love for Teddy that had nowhere to go.

I quickly realised that I had to get over the guilt that I had associated with the need to grow our family. In my mind, Teddy was always going to have younger siblings, but this just meant that they might appear sooner than expected as our path as a family had changed. Of course, as I write this now, we still haven't been fortunate enough to have had another successful pregnancy resulting in a sibling for Teddy. As the luck (or might I say bad luck) of the universe would have it, I have suffered with secondary fertility issues after losing our second pregnancy. I never, ever imagined that our road to recovery could have been made any more challenging, but it seems to have been. I had imagined myself by now with a baby in my arms and Teddy in my heart, but still we wait. It is easy sometimes to think the simpler route might be to just give up, to think that being a parent to a child who actually gets to come home might just not be within our grasp.

I just believe so strongly that it is. I can see it so vividly, and I believe that wonderful things will happen for our family. I think that belief is what keeps me going. It is what makes me thrive as Teddy's mother and enables me to keep a positive mindset about our future. I know that it is a challenge that many couples face after the loss of a child. People ask me why I don't get angry or upset that it hasn't happened for us yet. I won't lie – it does make me sad, of course it does. I am so desperate to be a mummy to a child who I actually get to push in a pram and feed and care for. I long to see my husband rocking our babies to sleep and carrying them on his front out on long walks with Boris. I keep those wishes in the forefront of my mind, and to me that keeps them within reach.

I like to think that we are all on our own path. Some people's paths will be more straightforward than others; some will face different challenges, with illness or loss of a parent early in their lives. Our path has seen us lose Teddy, and that has adjusted the course of where we are heading as a family and at what speed we can get there. However, it is our path, and I respect that. I shall continue to believe that it will happen for us, one day.

There are so many other elements to moving forward than expanding your family, of course. It's about gaining confidence again and calming the anxiety that loss might have brought upon you. It's about continuing to respect those changes and adaptations that we have made to our lives. We don't expect to spring back to normal anytime soon, and that's OK. We still don't book up our weekends with catch-ups or events, because sometimes we get to that weekend and we just can't do it. We still sometimes spend entire weekends without seeing anyone but each other and enjoying mundane things, like coffee in the garden or a long walk in the sunshine. We cancel on people at the last minute (yes, we are those annoying people) because sometimes we just can't face socialising or being away from home, or the outside world just starts to feel that little bit too noisy and overwhelming again. People understand – they don't berate us for it or think we aren't 'getting on with it'. Our friends and family respect that this is a major process, even though sometimes it feels like a very slow one, and that actually we have made some huge leaps and bounds in how we have dealt with life since Teddy died.

Let's not forget that there was a time when I couldn't walk around the park without freezing to the ground in a panic attack, I couldn't even walk around the aisles of Waitrose without suddenly bursting into inconsolable tears in the bread section. We have come so far, and some days we just need to reframe and refocus on that.

I think back on those days when I didn't want to open the shutters, when I couldn't swing my legs around the side of the bed to face the day, and I think about how I feel now as I am writing this. I remember the moment when I decided that I wouldn't be defeated by the universe and just curl into a ball. I am so proud that I didn't let that feeling win, that I chose to live life again and start to let the light back in. There comes a time, a moment, when you have to accept that, doesn't there? It's either that or just let everyone else in the world continue to have all of the fun while you accept that you're willing to sit on the sidelines and be a silent spectator for the remainder of time. No, not us.

As each month passes, we are getting stronger, and the normality of life is starting to creep back in. I wonder whether my body just wasn't ready to have another baby so soon after Teddy, and that is why we are where we are now. I guess I will never know. I do know that we are starting to enjoy our lives again though. We have begun to plan breaks away, and are making more plans for the house. All of these things actually feel exciting, too, and make me feel more like, well, me.

I guess I'll never understand why people feel the need to say that we should 'move on' from tragic events in our lives, or from losing loved ones. I feel so happy that we have started to strike a balance between keeping Teddy's memory and existence very much alive, while focusing on bringing happiness and enjoyment back into our lives. We might be Teddy's mummy and daddy, but we are also Elle and Nico, and I want us to be able to be both, without one not being in alignment with the other. I don't want the positivity of moving forward to be laced with any guilt that we are leaving Teddy behind. He'll always be with us – we are just moving forward, never on.

Dear Teddy

WELL, HERE IS A LETTER THAT I NEVER EXPECTED I
WOULD BE WRITING. A letter to you in a book about
your exit from this world, and how we survived. I
suppose I should start by saying thank you. Thank
you for choosing me to be your mummy, and for
giving me the strength each day to talk about you,
even to passing strangers.

You have made me feel so many things in life –
pride, happiness, the need to protect, pain, sorrow,
heartbreak, but the most intense of them all is love.
You have made me realise that love is the most
powerful emotion, because it is my love for you that
wipes the floor with the rest of those feelings, that

crashes through any barrier that life might put in its way, and that allows me to fill the hole that you have left in our lives. It is love that is in the forefront of my mind when I write about you, talk about you or refuse to be silenced when it comes to telling the world about you. Thank you for helping me to feel that love more than I feel your loss.

I had so many dreams for you, so many ideas about who you might become, what you might look and sound like. Would you have started to look more like me and less like your daddy? I often wonder if you'd love cereal as much as your daddy does, if you'd be an early riser or prefer to cuddle in bed with me. I think about how much our lives would have changed with you here, and what we might have done differently. I long to hear you say 'Mummy' just once, or to be able to look into your eyes. It's the little things I think about the most, the details of your life and personality that I'll never get to know. I spend a lot of time imagining them all and then un-doing it all in my mind as I know I'll never get them quite right. I try not to get too tangled up in them as I know that it's just a dream now that can't come true.

I think, so often, about those days that we spent

together with you in the hospital. You made me feel
so proud; I was bursting. I think about whether you
heard what I was saying to you – whether you felt it
when I put my finger into the clasp of your hand so
that you could hold it. I hope that you felt us there,
that you knew we were all rooting for you. I often
wonder what would have happened if my wish had
been granted and you had just woken up. It's the one
wish I ever made that I would give anything to come
true. I hope that you felt us all there when we said
goodbye and that you liked the story we read to you.
I didn't want you to be scared and I really hope you
felt that too.

The truth is, I don't want to be writing this book,
or this letter. I just want you. I want you to be here,
making a mess in the sitting room and rubbing
crumbs into the carpet as Boris desperately tries to
snuffle them up. I picture him following you around
the house like a little shadow; a mischievous duo. I
only ever wanted to be a 'normal mummy', that was
all, but you changed all of that for me. When you left
I became a mummy who had to survive, who has to
live out the rest of her days knowing that they will
never be filled with your laughter, or your 'firsts',
or all of the wonderful things that life held for you.

I had to say goodbye to the dreams of watching you taking toddler steps towards the surf on a beach in Cornwall, and of you learning to catch and throw a ball in the garden with Daddy. I would do anything for a sleepless night with you or a tantrum, I'd even take an afternoon at soft-play. All of those normal things feel like they are so far away now because you created a new normal for us.

Daddy and I talk about you so often. Your name is spoken every day in our home and your photos hang proudly on the walls. We miss you. Which sounds so silly, as we never even got to know you. We miss the ideas of the life we had planned with you in it, and we miss not being able to touch you, hold you or breathe you in.

I miss you wriggling around in my bump and letting me know you were there every so often with a big kick in the ribs. I so enjoyed that time we had together, just you and me. I wish I could have kept you safely in there forever; you see, that's what was keeping you here with us. I wish there had been an answer for you when you arrived, that it didn't have to end for us there. I hope that you know I would have done anything to protect you. I still will.

I don't ever want you to think that you'll be

forgotten, that you won't be our firstborn son, our eldest. I want you to be a big brother, and I want your siblings to know how much their brother is loved and thought about. I also want them to know how much you have taught me – about myself and about others. You have taught me to love fiercely and be passionate about what I believe in; you have taught me to look after myself and look after Daddy better. You have made me realise that life really is what we make of it, no matter how short our time here is, and that even the shortest of lives on this earth can have the hugest of impacts. You have taught me never to take anything for granted – never to expect an outcome just because we think that's the way it always turns out. To expect the unexpected and try to embrace it whatever happens. You have made me realise that we can face absolutely anything that life throws at us, when we have to.

You continue to make me so proud, every single day. All I can hope is that this book and the way I talk about you will make you just as proud of me. You, Teddy, are so very loved.

There is a quote from Peter Pan that I read over and over the week that you died. I remember feeling so sad because I wanted you to be able to see it too; I wanted it to bring you as much comfort as it had brought me, so that you wouldn't ever be scared or feel alone either. I felt that we had spent all of those months together and then that was it, we were just separated. So, I'll take this opportunity to share it with you now. . .

* * * ★ * * ★ * * ★ ★ * ★ ★

You know that place between sleep and awake, the one where you can still remember dreaming? That's where I will always love you, that's where I'll be waiting.

* * ★ ★ * * * * ★ * ★ ★ * ★ *

I just want you to know that this is all for you, my darling. It's *always*, all for you.

Sleep tight,
Mummy
xxx

Acknowledgements

THERE ARE SO MANY PEOPLE I NEED TO THANK FOR MAKING THIS BOOK COME TO FRUITION, AND I SIMPLY COULD NOT GO WITHOUT THANKING THEM. Firstly, Charlotte and her team at Rock my Family; who helped me share my writing and Teddy's story with a wider audience, and without whom I very much doubt I would have been given the opportunity to write this.

To the readers of my blog and Instagram posts; thank you for showing me that this was a subject that people wanted to engage with, and that people who haven't lost aren't scared to read about Teddy or the other beautiful babies gone too soon. Your kind comments and support always keep me writing and were definitely at the forefront of my mind as I wrote this.

A huge thank-you to Lauren, who has most certainly become a friend rather than my literary agent; thank you for trusting that people would want to read about Teddy and for helping me to see the potential of sharing his story in a book. Thank you for the lengthy phone calls of discussion and for always seeing and supporting what I wanted to achieve with this.

Thank you to Beth, Francesca and the wonderful team at Lagom for their dedication and attention to every detail in seeing this book through to completion. For their expert guidance and, most of all, for putting up with me on the occasions when I didn't agree! I hope you are all as proud of this as I am.

Thank you to Louise, Angie and Gretchen for their expertise in writing about their fields of work for this book in the hope it might also help others. For their continued support and friendship, and for helping me feel like 'me' again.

A special thank-you to my darling mum, Carol, for her entry in this book. If I am even half the mother to Teddy that you have been to us, then it will be my greatest achievement in this life.

Thank you also to Zoe and Amanda for their honest accounts and beautiful words. You have made this book so much more than a mother's account of loss, and I really hope that your entries bring comfort to those friends and families of bereaved parents who need to read your words.

Nico, you are my everything. Thank you for agreeing to write your piece for this, and for letting me keep all of my writing to myself until it was exactly perfect and ready for you to read. Your patience astounds me! I know that Teddy would be so very proud of his wonderful daddy, as am I. I love you.

To my Warrior Women (I know I have given you a chapter, but I feel like an extra thank-you is due!) – thank you for catching me when I fell, for allowing me a space to talk and for being the understanding voices that I needed to hear at my lowest ebb. Your friendships will always be the shining light that came from losing Teddy.

Lastly, to our friends and families, I cannot quite put into words how much your support, love and laughter has meant to both Nico and I since losing Teddy. I feel very fortunate to say that we have been lifted up by your kindness and never felt as though people couldn't talk about Teddy with us. Thank you for always speaking his name.

This Might Help

A LITTLE GUIDE OF RESOURCES THAT HAVE HELPED ME
– YOU MAY LIKE TO USE THEM TOO, IF YOU FEEL YOU
NEED THEM.

CHARITIES

Sands (Stillbirth & neonatal death charity)
Sands operates throughout the UK and works to support anyone affected by the death of a baby. It aims to improve the care bereaved parents receive and promote research to reduce the loss of babies' lives.
www.sands.org.uk

Tommy's
'We believe that parents need and deserve answers when their babies die. Tommy's exists to answer these questions.' Tommy's support parents after the loss of a baby and in future pregnancies, at their Rainbow Clinics.
www.tommys.org

The Mariposa Trust
The team at the 'Saying Goodbye' division of the Mariposa Trust are there to support bereaved parents, and offer them a place of peace and comfort after the loss of their baby.
www.mariposatrust.org
www.sayinggoodbye.org

Our Missing Peace
Set up and run by Nicole Bowles after the loss of her baby boy, Ben, in 2012, with the aim of unifying bereaved parents.

Our Missing Peace helps to simplify finding support for bereaved parents, regardless of circumstances. 'We want to make it easier for everyone to talk about child loss'.
www.ourmissingpeace.org

TOOLS

The Bees Knees Journal
A positivity journal created by Kelly Terranova, in the wake of her own family crisis (her mum's diagnosis of Huntington's Disease). Kelly has channelled her positive energy into a daily journal for people to enjoy and reflect on their lives.
www.thebeesknees.co

Yes Mum™ affirmation cards
I used the 'Strength' cards to get me through my toughest days. Hollie De Cruz (author and hypno-birthing coach) has also created cards for positive birthing, fertility, new mums, teens, self-love and a number of other uses. Place the pack on your bedside table, or anywhere you are likely to see them each day, and aim to turn over a new card every morning. They offer a quick and straightforward way to access the power of positive programming, and start each day with strength and self-assurance.

To shop for these cards and others, visit: www.yesmumcards.com.

FERTILITY AFTER LOSS

Many parents feel the need to begin trying for another baby as soon as possible. I have found Emma Cannon's expertise and approach to fertility (particularly fertility after loss) hugely helpful and inspiring. Emma is a UK leading expert in fertility, and writes books, leads talks and treats patients at her London clinic. www.emmacannon.co.uk

OTHER RESOURCES

If you are looking to access a registered acupuncturist for treatment in your local area, you can search for registered professionals using the British Acupuncture Council: www.acupuncture.org.uk.